920.02 CEILAN
Ceilán, Cynthia.
Thinning the herd : tales of
M   374970   05/23/11
New Albany-Floyd Co. Library

WITHDRAWN

FEB 0 1 2023

NAFC PUBLIC LIBRARY

Thinning the Herd

Thinning the Herd

Tales of the Weirdly Departed

CYNTHIA CEILÁN

MICHAEL O'MARA BOOKS LIMITED

First published in the United States in 2008 by The Lyons Press,
an imprint of The Globe Pequot Press
This edition published in Great Britain 2008 by Michael O'Mara Books Limited
9 Lion Yard
Tremadoc Road
London SW4 7NQ

Copyright © 2008 by Cynthia Ceilàn

All rights reserved. No part of this publication may be reproduced, stored in a
retrieval system, or transmitted by any means, without the prior permission in
writing of the publisher, nor be otherwise circulated in any form of binding or
cover other than that in which it is published and without a similar condition
including this condition being imposed on the subsequent purchaser.

A CIP catalogue record for this book is available from the British Library.
Papers used by Michael O'Mara Books Limited are natural, recyclable products
made from wood grown in sustainable forests. The manufacturing processes
conform to the environmental regulations of the country of origin.

ISBN: 978-1-84317-291-8

1 3 5 7 9 10 8 6 4 2

Printed and bound in England by Clays Ltd, St Ives plc

www.mombooks.com

For Mike and Jeff

Table of Contents

Acknowledgments		ix
Introduction		xi
CHAPTER 1:	Oops	1
CHAPTER 2:	Inescapable Destiny	13
CHAPTER 3:	How the Mighty Have Fallen	23
CHAPTER 4:	Death's Little Ironies	43
CHAPTER 5:	So Sexy It Hurts	53
CHAPTER 6:	Rampage of Angels	63
CHAPTER 7:	It Seemed Like a Good Idea at the Time	73
CHAPTER 8:	Play Ball!	89
CHAPTER 9:	Better Luck Next Time	101
CHAPTER 10:	When the Fur Flies	111
CHAPTER 11:	Just Plain Weird	123
CHAPTER 12:	Deaths Foretold	135
CHAPTER 13:	Hmm	143
Sources		151

Acknowledgments

Thank you, Holly Rubino of The Lyons Press, for letting your inner ghoul come out and play.

Thank you, Mom, for not sending the police after me, like you promised, when I ran away to college.

Thank you, Dad, for the gift of laughter, and for being there, no matter what.

Thank you, Mike and Jeff, for being my little brothers. I have observed your weirdness from up close for many years. You, more than anyone else in the world, make me feel normal.

And thank you, Christopher, for your support, your encouragement, your love, and – most especially – for being careful not to step on Pee-Pee Petie.

Introduction

I WANT TO DIE IN MY SLEEP LIKE MY GRANDFATHER, NOT
YELLING AND SCREAMING LIKE THE PASSENGERS IN HIS CAR.

Will Shriner

THOSE OF US who embrace a certain fascination with particularly odd ways of dying tend to shrug off suggestions that we might be a little bit nuts. Deep down, however, we fear our friends and loved ones may be right. We nevertheless find solace, and perhaps even a little pride, in knowing that we manage to live and work among the normal people, very often undetected. We have families, jobs, mortgages, and occasionally, we serve on juries.

Death, to most of us, is the sort of thing that only happens to other people, namely the very dumb, the very crazy, and the very unlucky. We, of course, are not other people. We are smart, and we are sane. We are going to live forever. And then one day, when we are 117 years old, we will go to sleep for a long, long time and, when we wake up, the icky part will be over.

CHAPTER

1

OOPS

IF ALL ELSE FAILS, IMMORTALITY CAN ALWAYS BE
ASSURED BY SPECTACULAR ERROR.
John Kenneth Galbraith (1908-2006)

I WONDER HOW *often, in the normal course of any ordinary day, each of us comes* this close *to meeting the Reaper without ever realizing it. I'm sure I've been lucky more often than I will ever know. The same is probably true for most people. For others, not so much.*

The clown act of Jo-Jo and Mr. Ollie was pretty standard circus fare in the early 1900s. A big mean guy (Jo-Jo) terrorizes a hapless little guy (Mr. Ollie).

In real life, Jo-Jo and Ollie were good friends. They were also avid drinking buddies. One night, after a few too many preshow tipples, Jo-Jo forgot to put on his wooden wig. At the climax of the act, when Mr. Ollie bests his nemesis by hitting him on the head with a hatchet, Jo-Jo fell dead on the sawdust for real.

Circus clowns immediately descended on the scene from all corners of the tent to carry Jo-Jo out on a stretcher before anyone in the audience could realize the performers' tragic error. Unfortunately, they grabbed a prop stretcher by mistake. When they lifted the poles and ran, Jo-Jo stayed behind on the ground, still gushing blood from his head, still dead.

A distraught Mr. Ollie ran around the centre ring of the big top, crying and screaming, and tripped over his own big floppy shoes. He suffered only minor injuries in the fall.

The secret code for prompting the circus ushers to clear the tent during an emergency called for the band to play 'Stars and Stripes Forever.' Instead, they played 'Strike Up the Band.' Everyone rose to their feet, cheering maniacally.

It was far and away the greatest moment in the history of Jo-Jo and Mr. Ollie's clowning career.

❧

John Lewis of Minsterworth, Gloucester set out to do a little gardening one fine day in the summer of 1999. He snipped some shrubs, weeded his garden, and raked up the debris into an average-sized pile. He poured some gasoline over it to get a good bonfire going, then lit a match. The ensuing explosion engulfed most of John's clothing in flames, but he was able to run toward a nearby river to put himself out. Unfortunately, he couldn't swim. John drowned and was dragged several miles downstream. His body was found two weeks later, clad only in socks and shoes.

❧

Before the invention of anesthesia, speed was of the essence in performing surgery. Dr. Robert Liston (1794–1847) was arguably the fastest scalpel on record. He is reputed to have been able to amputate and suture a limb in thirty seconds flat. Unfortunately, accuracy was not as big a priority for the good doctor. He once amputated a man's leg – and his testicles – in a single swipe of the knife.

Liston's most infamous claim to fame, however, is being the only surgeon on record to have a 300 percent mortality rate during a single operation. He accidentally cut off the fingers of his surgical assistant, who later died of septic shock. Liston also slashed through the coat tails of a colleague observing the operation, who died of fright on the spot, thinking that Liston had severed his vital organs. The patient survived the procedure, but later died of gangrene.

If Guinness had a record for the world's most accident-prone people, Frances and Michael Mosey of Scotland would surely be strong contenders for the title. Frances's run of bad luck began at the age of five, when she fell from a table and shot a bamboo cane through the roof of her mouth. Other accidents in Frances's astonishingly long life include crashing her bike into a concrete lamppost, getting her legs trapped in the back of her father's tractor, falling into a six-foot pothole and breaking both legs, breaking a toe when she dropped a sewing machine on it, fracturing her skull when a hospital ceiling tile fell on her head while she was recovering from a hernia operation, fracturing an ankle while buying ice cream for her granddaughter, and slicing off a finger – which her dog promptly ate.

Until Michael Mosey met Frances, he had led a pretty normal life. Afterward, things changed. Over the years, Michael fell through a greenhouse – on three separate occasions. He also cut his forehead on a glass coffee table, fell off a chair and broke his back, broke his right leg after accidentally standing on a puppy, was partially blinded after drinking a bottle of tainted black-market vodka, and got run over by a car while riding home on his new motorcycle. The driver of the car that hit him was, of course, his wife, Frances.

Left to his own devices, Michael might have lived to recover from many more accidents. Sadly, his streak was broken in 2003 when, at the age of fifty-seven, an intruder broke into his home and beat him to death.

✿

An unidentified young man from the port city of Haiphong found an interesting-looking tennis ball in a ditch one day in 2002. When he used it to play a game of catch with some friends, the ball exploded, killing him and injuring six others. The tennis ball turned out to be a small American bomb left over from the Vietnam War.

✿

In 2006, Sharffe Williams from Oakland California, was caught on videotape robbing a liquor store. He almost got away with it, too. When he put his gun back into the waistband of his pants, he accidentally shot himself in the leg. Police found his body at the end of a trail of blood, not far from the scene of the robbery.

✿

Director Boris Sagal was so immersed in his work during the filming of the 1982 television miniseries *World War III* that he didn't notice how close he was to danger. He was walking backward while explaining his vision of one particular scene and stepped directly into the path of a spinning helicopter rotor blade. He was hacked to pieces.

❧

Jean-Baptiste Lully was an impassioned seventeenth-century composer and conductor. He got a little carried away one day while conducting a religious concert. Lully stabbed himself in the foot with his baton, which at the time was more like a staff, and later died of gangrene.

❧

On Election Day, 2006, Sam Duncan handily won his bid for a county board seat in Monroe, North Carolina despite one minor flaw: he had been dead for more than a month. Election officials knew Duncan was dead, but didn't tell the voters. 'We are instructed that it's not our job to do that,' explained elections director Shirley Secrest.

❧

Péter Vályi, the finance minister of Hungary, knew pretty much nothing about the production of steel. Nevertheless, he visited a steelworks factory in 1973 and performed an inspection that was largely ceremonial. When he stepped up to get a better look at a blast furnace, he fell right in.

❧

Daniel Wright of Gary, Indiana donned a bulletproof vest and asked a friend to shoot him with a .20-gauge shotgun. The vest turned out to be a flak jacket, not a projectile repellent.

Thinning the Herd

꙳

By most accounts, French composer Charles-Valentin Alkan (1813–1888) was a man of great faith. To prove it, he wrote phenomenally difficult piano pieces. While reaching for a volume near the top of his bookcase, he lost his balance, which caused the bookcase to topple over on top of him. He survived the fall, but was killed by the avalanche of books.

꙳

After not hearing from Marina Weber for several days, her family reported the petite 38-year-old woman missing. Eleven days after filing the missing persons report, Marina's mother and sister noticed a strange odor in the house. Following their noses, they found Marina wedged behind a six-foot bookcase. She had fallen head first and become trapped behind the bookcase when she tried to adjust her television set, which sat on the top shelf.

꙳

Ormer Locklear was an actor and fearless stunt pilot in the early days of flight and movie-making. He once calmly walked onto his aircraft while in mid-flight to plug a rag into the opening of the radiator when the cap blew off. While filming a night scene in the 1920 silent film *The Skywayman*, he crash-landed into a group of oil rigs parked at DeMille Airfield in California. The film crew had forgotten to turn on the runway lights.

❧

Dag Hammarskjöld, the UN secretary general, was on a plane with fifteen others in 1961. They were on their way to a peace mission in the Congo. While flying over Zambia (formerly Rhodesia), someone on the ground fired a warning shot to alert the pilot of a possible attack by Katanga rebels. The bullet hit the plane, causing it to crash in the jungle.

❧

In June 1988, a Ukrainian man died after consuming tainted liquor he had obtained on the black market. At his funeral, ten of his mourners also died. They had each taken a drink from the same supply of alcohol.

❧

Nguyen Van Hung of Cambodia was known to millions as the amazing 'Hung Electric.' Hung appeared on numerous television programs demonstrating his ability to withstand high-voltage electric shocks. He died in his home in 2006 when he forgot to turn off the power before repairing a generator.

❧

Before a congregation of 800 worshippers, Baptist minister Kyle Lake of Waco, Texas was electrocuted when he reached for a microphone while standing in the church's baptismal pool in 2005.

Thinning the Herd

David Frazer survived being thrown from his car when it rolled over several times on a New Zealand highway. As he lay sprawled in the middle of the road, grateful to be alive, he was run over by an oncoming trailer truck. The truck had swerved to avoid Frazer's overturned car.

After being notified by concerned friends, police entered the Liverpool home of William and Emily Shortis in 1903. There they found slim William near death, trapped under his 224-pound wife Emily. Three days earlier, William had been following his wife up the stairs when she lost her balance and fell backward. Emily died instantly of head injuries. William died shortly after being rescued.

In 1997, Karen Wetterhahn, a young scientist who had quietly achieved great success and respect in her field, was studying a man-made chemical called dimethylmercury. She took all the necessary precautions: gloves, goggles, a pristine work environment. A drop of the chemical fell on her gloved hand and she promptly washed it off and proceeded with her work. What Ms. Wetterhahn had not yet had a chance to discover was that the chemical could pass through latex without making a visible hole. She died of mercury poisoning a year later.

❧

In 1989, a false alarm indicating engine failure prompted the crew to bail out of a Soviet MiG-23 fighter jet that had just escaped from Poland. They put the plane on autopilot, put on their parachutes, and jumped out. They forgot to take with them the Belgian teenager they had just rescued.

❧

The brilliant author, social critic, and religious leader, Thomas Merton, was lecturing in Bangkok in 1968. The oppressive heat and the man's advanced age quickly tired him, so he retired to his room immediately after the talk. He took a shower and then, still damp, went to turn on a small electric fan near his bed. About an hour later, a nun found him lying on the floor, naked, and on his back with the fan buzzing on his chest. He was still sizzling from the electric shock that had killed him.

❧

When fire consumed a Dutch hospital in 2006, the surgical team had no time to take anything with them when they fled, not even the 69-year-old woman they had just strapped to the operating table. The woman had been given a mild sedative, but was still wide awake when the last of the operating room staff ran screaming from the room.

❧

In 1927, famed dancer and lover of long scarves, Isadora Duncan, got into a convertible automobile and said, 'Farewell, my friends! I go to glory!' The scarf she was wearing became entangled in the wheel of the car as it drove off, strangling her and breaking her neck.

❧

Word got out that rehearsals were going ahead for the funeral of the Queen Mother in 1993, prompting the Australian press to report a little too soon that she had already died. The Queen Mother, in fact, lived to see the new millennium, dying peacefully in her bed at the age of 101. Funeral rehearsals were conducted every six months or so in order to make the final spectacular tribute appear perfectly spontaneous. For the long-lived Queen Mother, the rehearsals went on for decades.

❧

Newspapers all over the world printed the obituary of Dorothy Southworth Ritter in August 2001. The star of 1940s western movies, known also as Dorothy Fay, was the widow of singing cowboy Tex Ritter, and the mother of actor John Ritter. Ms. Ritter had been living in a nursing home after suffering a stroke. When a friend stopped by to visit, he was told Ms. Ritter was gone. The friend alerted the media, which put the obituary machine in motion. Ms. Ritter had, in fact, 'gone' to another room in the facility.

John J. Taylor of Wisconsin considered himself a very lucky man. While serving in the army during World War II, his plane was shot down in a round of friendly fire. Although badly burned, he was able to pull himself and three other men onto a raft, and all were saved. After the war, Taylor dedicated himself to enjoying the great outdoors. He broke his back on a ski jump, and broke it again when he jumped over a tennis net. Once, while hunting, the goose he shot fell from the sky and hit him in the chest, shaking loose cartilage in his sternum that left him with breathing problems for a year. On a fly-fishing expedition, he slipped and fell into the Missouri River, but was pulled to safety by rescuers. In his later years, Taylor ran a small business selling firewood to his friends, until one day in 2005, a tree fell on top of him. After eighty-five long and wonderful years, John Taylor had finally had his last accident.

In 2003, ten people died and more than seventy were injured in Santa Monica, California, when 89-year-old George Russell Weller's car plowed through a busy farmers' market. His attorneys called it 'pedal error.' Prosecutors claimed that Weller looked at what he had done, shrugged his shoulders, and said, 'Oops.'

2

INESCAPABLE DESTINY

I'D RATHER GET MY BRAINS BLOWN OUT IN THE WILD
THAN WAIT IN TERROR AT THE SLAUGHTERHOUSE.
Craig Volk

I DON'T KNOW *if there really is such a thing as predestination,
or if it's simply that our greatest fears are the very things most likely
to become self-fulfilling prophecies. But maybe, just maybe, some of us
end up getting killed by the very thing we've been avoiding all our lives.
I find that kind of funny.*

Young film starlet Linda Darnell developed a severe case of pyrophobia after having been burned on several occasions during film shoots in the 1940s. She had also at one time suffered serious burns in a car accident. At the age of forty-one, while she was watching one of her old films on late-night television, her house caught fire. Darnell was burned over 90 percent of her body. She died the next day.

During the final test flight of a new Douglas DC-7B airliner in 1957, the plane ran almost head-on into a US Air Force F-89J Scorpion jet fighter. The pilots were able to swerve and missed each other, but they lost control of their respective planes and crashed. One of those killed was a copilot named Archie R. Twitchell. He was an actor who appeared in more than seventy films, including *I Wanted Wings* and *Among the Living*.

Flaming pieces of the wreckage fell onto a junior high school playground. One of the three students killed on the ground was a good friend of Richard Valenzuela, who would skyrocket to fame as rock-and-roll singer Ritchie Valens less than two years later. Having witnessed the carnage firsthand Valens developed a horrendous fear of airplanes. The one and only time he ever got into a plane, it too crashed, killing him, Buddy Holly, J. P. Richardson (also known as The Big Bopper), and everyone else on board.

A pilot who survived a helicopter crash in the mountains of southwest Colombia in 1996 was thrilled to see the rescuers who arrived to save him from certain death. He was killed when he fell out of the rescue chopper.

A sixty-year-old man identified only as Czeslaw B. from the Polish village of Kosianka-Trojanówka had an overwhelming fear of burglars. He booby-trapped every entrance and exit in his house, including the garage, which he outfitted with two homemade guns. He was killed in 1996 while opening the garage doors.

Texas pioneer Josiah P. Wilbarger was scalped by Comanches in 1833, but survived the attack. Despite his exposed skull, he lived well for eleven more years, until he bumped his head against a low beam in his cotton gin.

The 1955 film *Rebel Without a Cause* was the story of troubled teens caught in a violent world of their own creation and their inability to connect with the older generation. Four of the movie's stars died tragically at a young age: James Dean died in a car crash. Natalie Wood drowned. Sal Mineo was murdered. Nick Adams overdosed on drugs.

The Flying ELVI is a daredevil skydiving team of Elvis Presley impersonators who rent themselves out for grand openings and all manner of over-the-top celebrations. Their act involves a dazzling combination of smoke trails, pyrotechnic fireworks, precision maneuvers, and the occasional splattered Elvis.

In 1996, one of the ELVI was blown off course as the troupe descended onto Boston Harbor. That Elvis died of his injuries. During a show in Montana in 2006, another Elvis broke most of his bones, including his pelvis, when he misjudged the landing and hit a concrete parking lot at 50 miles per hour. Yet another Elvis, who had given up the group because he found the experience thrilling but too dangerous, died in a plane crash in Ohio in 2003.

Comic book illustrator Dave Cockrum died in bed in 2006 wearing Superman pajamas and covered in a Batman blanket. He was cremated dressed in a Green Lantern shirt.

CNN announced to the world that rock musician Kurt Cobain had died of a drug overdose in Rome in March 1994. The news agency had to retract the story, of course, but not for long. Cobain blew his own brains out in Seattle just one month later. In his suicide note, he quoted Neil Young: 'Better to burn out than to fade away.'

❧

Actor Jeffrey Hunter had a lot of trouble getting cast in other roles after playing Jesus Christ in the 1961 film *King of Kings*. He acted mostly in small European productions and on television. In the meantime, he suffered a series of head injuries. He was hit by an exploding prop, was accidentally karate-chopped in the head, and had at least one seizure. A few days after being diagnosed with a displaced vertebra at the age of forty-two, he collapsed while climbing a flight of stairs in his house and hit his head again, this time fatally.

❧

During the filming of the Chuck Norris action film *Braddock: Missing in Action III* in the Philippines, a helicopter crash killed three extras. Two years later, Chuck returned to the Philippines to shoot another movie, *Delta Force 2*. This time, a helicopter crash killed five people. Apparently having learned nothing from their first tragic experience, the crew used a helicopter that had been repossessed by a bank and had been sitting in the hot tropical climate for several years.

❧

Mark Twain was born in 1835 as Halley's Comet passed close to the Earth. He felt certain all his life that, because he had come in with Halley, he would also go out with it. Sure enough, he died in 1910, when the comet was once again visible from Earth.

❧

King Henry II of France arranged for a three-day jousting tournament in 1559 to take place during his daughter's wedding celebration. In a famous quatrain issued one year before, Nostradamus had warned the king not to engage in jousts or combats of any kind:

The Lion shall overcome the old
On the field of war in a single combat (duelle);
He will pierce his eyes in a cage of gold.
This is the first of two lappings, then he dies a cruel death.

Ignoring the warning, the King went forward with his plans and engaged in a joust with Gabriel Montgomery, a captain with the Scottish Guard. Montgomery's lance tip broke off in the soft golden grille of King Henry's helmet, piercing his eye and lodging in his brain. The King died eleven days later.

❧

The first Canadian to conquer Niagara Falls in a barrel was a man named Karel Soucek. He took the plunge in July of 1984 and survived. He then went on tour demonstrating his technique. While re-creating the drop from a platform inside the Houston Astrodome, the barrel hit the edge of the water tank. Soucek was killed on impact.

John Wilkes Booth, Abraham Lincoln's assassin, enlisted in the Confederate Army only so that he could witness the hanging of abolitionist John Brown. As soon as that was done, he went back to his career as a mediocre actor. However, he continued his affiliation with sympathizers of the Confederacy, and believed he would ultimately prevail as a hero of the cause.

After shooting the president, Booth jumped off the theatre balcony and broke his leg when he landed on the floor below. He managed to limp outside and mount his horse, and headed toward Maryland. He stopped at several places along the way, seeking sanctuary and medical assistance, but was repeatedly turned away by his fellow Confederates. Interestingly, it was a black farmer who helped him cross the Zekiah Swamp to the home of Samuel Cox, who also turned him away.

Booth finally found refuge in a barn owned by southerner Richard Garrett. Authorities closed in and set fire to some hay to smoke the assassin out. When he emerged from the barn, an officer raised his gun, aiming for Booth's arm. Booth made a jerking movement just as the officer pulled the trigger. The bullet hit Booth in the head, in very nearly the same spot as where Booth had shot the president.

As he lay dying, Booth uttered these words: 'Tell Mother I died for my country. Useless! Useless!'

꘍

Playwright George Bernard Shaw once said, 'Life does not cease to be funny when people die.' He died in 1950 at the age of ninety-four, when he fell out of an apple tree.

꘍

Upon hearing of his father's suicide in 1928, Ernest Hemingway skulked away in disgust, calling the man a coward. The elder Hemingway had shot himself with an heirloom Civil War revolver, given to him by his own father. Three decades later, Hemingway himself would put a 12-gauge shotgun in his mouth and pull the trigger. In the decades that followed, more Hemingways would perish in strange and certain ways. Ernest's sister, Ursula, died of a drug overdose in 1966 after finding out she had cancer. His brother, Leicester, shot himself in 1982. Hemingway's famous supermodel granddaughter, Margaux, died in 1995 after ingesting a lethal dose of prescription medication. Hemingway's youngest son, Gregory, a former doctor, author, and transsexual, was found dead in 2001, in his cell in a woman's prison, after having been arrested for indecent exposure in Florida.

꘍

A scene in the 1974 film *Dirty Mary Crazy Larry* had to be rewritten when actor Vic Morrow refused to get into a helicopter. 'I have a premonition that I'm going to get killed in a helicopter crash,' he said. Ten years later, Morrow was hacked to pieces by a helicopter rotor during the making of *Twilight Zone: The Movie*.

❧

Magician and comedian Tommy Cooper entertained British audiences for many years with his deliberately bumbling illusions and quasi-death-defying feats. During a live television broadcast in 1984 at Her Majesty's Theatre, London, Cooper dropped dead of a heart attack in the middle of his show. The crowd cheered. They thought it was part of the act.

❧

Austrian composer Arnold Schoenberg suffered horrendous panic attacks because of his triskaidekaphobia (fear of the number thirteen). He was born on September 13, 1874. He died of fright on Friday the 13th, in July of 1951. At the time of his death, he was 76 years old (7 + 6 = 13).

❧

Composer Anton von Webern left Vienna during World War II, believing he would be safer in Mittersill, Austria. While standing on the veranda of his son-in-law's house, he was accidentally shot by a drunk American soldier.

❧

The soul singer and songwriter Donnie Hathaway loved leaning out the window of his seventeen-story apartment in Chicago, preaching and singing to the crowds below. He also liked preaching from hotel windows whenever he was on tour, and was frequently asked to leave the premises. In January 1979, Hathaway leaned out a little too far and fell to his death from the fifteenth floor of New York's Essex Hotel. It is unclear whether he fell, jumped, or was pushed.

3

HOW THE MIGHTY
HAVE FALLEN

I AM READY TO MEET MY MAKER. WHETHER MY MAKER IS PREPARED
FOR THE GREAT ORDEAL OF MEETING ME IS ANOTHER MATTER.
Winston Churchill (1874–1965)

IT'S NOT THAT *I like to snigger when I hear that some famously bombastic
fool has met an appropriately embarrassing end. Well, yes, I do, a little.
We are all, in that final moment, equally capable of meeting death with
great dignity, with one last fabulous flourish of panache, or with a great
big messy pant-load of fear for somebody else to clean up later.*

In 1779, the natives of the Sandwich Islands so loved and admired their 'discoverer' Captain James Cook that they stabbed him several dozen times, put him on a big stick, roasted him, and served him for dinner. The portions they did not eat that night were salted and preserved as leftovers. Afterward, they took back their islands' original name: Hawaii.

João Rodrigues Cabrilho was the swashbuckling sixteenth-century explorer who discovered California. In a dashing display of bravado, he leapt from one of his ships, sword in hand to join in the fight against the hostile natives. He broke his leg in the fall and died of gangrene.

Al Capone, arguably the most notorious American gangster of all time, was a longtime member of the FBI's Ten Most Wanted list. His involvement in the murders of countless rivals and perceived enemies, illegal gambling, prostitution, and bootlegging was the stuff of legend. Despite numerous attempts to bring him to justice for his crimes, he was ultimately prosecuted and found guilty of tax evasion. While serving time in a maximum security prison, he died of syphilis.

Thinning the Herd

❧

Attila the Hun was one of history's most notorious villains. By the year AD 450, he had conquered all of Asia, destroying every village in his path and pillaging the countryside from Mongolia to the outer edges of the Russian Empire. He died of a nosebleed on his wedding night.

❧

Pope Formosus, head of the Catholic Church between AD 891 and AD 896, was one of relatively few people tried and convicted in a court of law after they were already dead. Formosus's political enemies exhumed his corpse, propped him up on a throne, dressed him in full papal regalia, and tried him on charges of perjury and other offenses. A church deacon answered for the corpse. Formosus's holiness was declared invalid and all of his acts as Pope were nullified. They even cut off his consecration fingers so he couldn't bless anyone in the afterlife. Formosus's corpse was then thrown into a grave, but later pulled out and thrown into the River Tiber.

❧

The last thing singer Jackie Wilson knew for certain was that he was doing what he loved. He suffered a stroke and a heart attack while performing on stage in 1967, singing his greatest hit, 'Lonely Teardrops.' He died eight years later, having never regained consciousness.

It took W. C. Fields a rather long time to die. Years of boozing had decimated his liver, as well as many of his other internal organs. Fields's last coherent words tidily summed up the famous curmudgeon's attitudes about everything: 'God damn the whole friggin' world and everyone in it but you, Carlotta!' This made the love of his life, Carlotta, very happy indeed. His wife, Hattie, on the other hand was none too pleased.

❧

Three things distinguished the short reign of Alexander I of Greece: he ascended to the throne when his father abdicated in 1917, he became king before his older brother (it usually works the other way around), and his role was mostly ceremonial (the prime minister wielded the real power). However, Alexander will most likely be remembered for the manner in which he died: He was attacked by his gardener's monkey. The bite wounds became infected, and Alexander died of sepsis.

❧

At the start of the French Revolution in the late eighteenth century, Thomas de Mahay, Marquis de Favras, was tricked into making arrangements to help King Louis XVI and Marie Antoinette escape the country, and then sentenced to hang for treason. A court clerk handed him the official death sentence. The marquis read it carefully and said to the clerk, 'I see that you have made three spelling mistakes.'

꩜

After having ridden on horseback for several hours in the cold and snow, George Washington returned home exhausted and with a severe case of laryngitis. He was given a concoction of molasses, vinegar, and butter and told to gargle. A preparation of dried beetles was also placed on his throat, and four and a half liters of blood were extracted within a twenty-four-hour period (bloodletting was still a very common practice in the 1700s). George Washington had survived the American Revolution, the nation's first presidency, and innumerable armed and political battles, but died of his own doctor's ministrations.

꩜

After having been shot in battle, Mexican revolutionary Pancho Villa turned to a journalist who was nearby and shouted, 'Don't let it end like this! Tell them I said something!'

꩜

In the year AD 260, the Roman Emperor Valerian was defeated in battle and captured by the Persians. King Shapur I turned him into a human footstool. After many years of this humiliation, Valerian offered the king a large ransom for his release. In response, Shapur had molten gold poured down Valerian's throat. Shapur then had Valerian skinned, and the skin stuffed with straw and preserved as a trophy in the main Persian temple. Only after Persia's defeat in their last war with Rome 350 years later was Valerian's skin cremated and given proper burial.

❧

George Plantagenet, Duke of Clarence, was sentenced to death in 1478 for conspiring with the Burgundians against his brothers, King Edward IV and Richard III of England. George was secretly executed in the Tower of London, drowned in a barrel of wine.

❧

General John Sedgwick, Union commander, was killed in battle during the US Civil War. His last words were, 'They couldn't hit an elephant at this dist—'

❧

Ancient Greek dramatist, Aeschylus, who once wrote, 'O Death the Healer, scorn thou not . . . Pain lays not its touch upon a corpse,' was killed when a giant vulture-like bird dropped a turtle on his head.

❧

Ben Klassen was at one time a Florida state legislator. He was also the man who invented the electric can opener. However, he achieved his greatest success in 1973, when he founded the Church of the Creator and became a huge magnet for neo-Nazis and white supremacists from all over the world. When one of his followers killed a Persian Gulf War veteran in 1993, the family of the murdered soldier filed suit against the church. Klassen sold the compound, then blew his own brains out.

❧

Poet and grammarian Philetas of Cos is said to have died of insomnia in 270 BC. He drove himself crazy trying to figure out the Liar Paradox: 'I am lying now. This statement is false.'

❧

In 1799, Constantine Hangerli, Prince of Wallachïa, was arrested by a Kapucu and a Moor, and sentenced to multiple executions. He was strangled, shot, stabbed, and decapitated, all in rapid succession.

❧

Obituary writers at *The Daily Telegraph* jumped the gun a bit when they reported that Cockie Hoogterp had been killed in a car accident. Cockie was the second wife of Baron Bror Blixen-Finecke. It was, in fact, the baron's third wife who had been killed the crash. His first wife, Karen von Blixen-Finecke (also known as the author Isak Dinesen), had died her own weird death decades earlier.

Cockie began returning all of her bills marked deceased and demanded that *The Telegraph* publish the following statement: 'Mrs. Hoogterp wishes it to be known that she has not yet been screwed in her coffin.'

When Cockie really did die, her obituary in *The Telegraph* said of her, 'Few women, other than the very rich, can have survived into the late 1980s without ever having boiled an egg or made her own bed.'

❧

In 121 BC, the Roman Senate wanted a powerful public speaker named Gaius Gracchus dead. The Senate set as a bounty the weight of Gracchus's head in gold. One of the co-conspirators, Septimuleius, decapitated Gracchus, scooped out his brains, and filled the skull with molten lead. Septimuleius was paid in full: 17 pounds of gold.

❧

Pope Clement VII died in 1534 after eating the death cap mushroom. It is widely believed he was deliberately poisoned.

❧

Pedro de Valdivia, the dreaded sixteenth-century Spanish conquistador, was captured and killed by Native Americans. They poured molten gold down his throat to satisfy his thirst for their treasures.

❧

Zachary Taylor, twelfth president of the United States, while attending the laying of the cornerstone of the Washington Monument on an exceptionally hot and humid Fourth of July, quickly consumed large quantities of iced milk, cold cherries, and pickled cucumbers. He died of uncontrollable diarrhea five days later.

❧

Beloved Empress Elisabeth (Sissi) of Austria was long considered one of the world's most beautiful women. She sustained the image through decades-long starvation diets and obsessive exercise, which resulted in severe malnutrition, depression, and suicidal fantasies. While she was strolling on the promenade along Lake Geneva in 1898, a crazed Italian anarchist stabbed her with a needle-thin file. She had been so severely strapped into her corset that she hardly noticed. She walked a dozen or so steps and asked, 'What happened to me?' And then she died.

❧

It seemed that the enemies of the last Tsar of Russia would never succeed in assassinating Grigory Rasputin, the Russian mystic, friend, and advisor to the Romanovs. The conspirators poisoned him, bludgeoned him, and shot him in the head, lungs, and liver. Rasputin was still alive when he was dumped in the Neva River. He drowned when he became trapped under the ice.

❧

Barcelona's superstar architect, Antoni Gaudí, was run over by a streetcar in 1926. He was very shabbily dressed at the time, and cab drivers refused requests from bystanders to take 'the poor vagabond' to the hospital. Gaudí died in a pauper's clinic a few days later. When it was discovered that the 'bum' was in fact the venerated Gaudí, police fined all the cab drivers.

❧

President James Garfield lay dying after having been shot by a would-be assassin. Alexander Graham Bell rushed to the president's side with one of his new inventions: the metal detector. It did not occur to the brilliant inventor until much later that the device could not tell the difference between a bullet and a bedspring. Garfield died of septicemia (an infection in the blood) after having suffered multiple incisions at the hands of his doctor, who kept opening Garfield up in all the wrong places, guided by Bell and his machine in search of the bullet.

❧

Two and a half years after the death of Oliver Cromwell in 1658, he was exhumed, tried, found guilty of treason, and executed all over again. Cromwell's corpse was hanged, and then decapitated for good measure. His body was thrown into a pit, and his head stuck on a pole. The moldering head-on-a-stick was on display in front of Westminster Abbey for more than twenty-five years.

For the next three centuries, Cromwell's head would exchange hands repeatedly as a gruesomely sought-after collector's item. It was finally bequeathed to Cambridge University in 1960, where it was buried near Sidney Sussex Chapel.

❧

Distraught over the severe criticism he was receiving for his novel, *Finnegan's Wake,* author James Joyce asked before dying, 'Really? Does no one understand?'

❧

Pope John XXI was an ophthalmologist before entering religious life. In his first year as Pope, he ordered a special laboratory built on the grounds of the Vatican so that he could work in relative peace and quiet. During construction in 1277, the building collapsed on top of him, ending his short reign.

❧

In the 1960s race between the United States and the Soviet Union to develop the first intercontinental ballistic missile, Soviet Red Army marshal Mitrofan Nedelin gruffly dismissed his technicians' warnings and ordered them to forge ahead with preparations to launch the first R-16 rocket. Nedelin set up a chair at the launchpad to better oversee the operations. As predicted, the missile exploded, instantly incinerating Nedelin and everyone else in the immediate area. They were the lucky ones. Dozens of others were also killed in the explosion, but most of them died slow, miserable deaths because they were a little farther away.

❧

Henrik Ibsen was a brilliant and prolific playwright until he suffered a stroke in 1900 at the age of seventy-two. After that, his marriage was described as 'joyless' and his thinking 'cloudy.' As the end of his life neared, a friend who came to visit asked his housekeeper how Ibsen was holding up. The housekeeper said he was feeling a little better, to which Ibsen replied, 'On the contrary!' and died.

❧

The Crown Prince Dipendra of Nepal was not particularly pleased with his parents' choice for a bride. He was madly in love with another woman. He entered the billiards room after dinner one night in 2001, drunk and heavily armed. He went on a rampage and massacred most of the royal family. Dipendra himself died four days later from wounds he received from the palace guards trying to subdue him. Officials of the royal court insisted that all of the killings were accidental.

❧

At a meeting with his advisors, Sobhuza II, King of Swaziland abruptly stopped the discussion and dismissed everyone from the room, except for his minister of health. Sobhuza said to the man, 'I am going.' The minister asked, 'Where?' Sobhuza smiled, waved good-bye, and dropped dead.

❧

The ancient Greek philosopher Socrates was found guilty of corrupting the morals of minors and was sentenced to death by poison. Before taking the drink of hemlock, Socrates turned to his friend, Crito, and said, 'I owe Asclepius a cock. Will you remember to pay the debt?'

❧

Albert Einstein spoke his last words on his deathbed, but we will never know what they were. His nurse didn't speak German.

❧

Simón Bolívar, the great soldier and statesman who successfully led the revolution against Spanish rule in South America, died on a hammock while visiting a friend in 1830. Shortly before expiring, he commented, 'The three biggest fools that have ever lived are Christ, Don Quixote, and me.'

❧

While sleeping in a dark room, the outlaw Billy the Kid suddenly sat up and asked, 'Who's there?' To which sheriff Pat Garrett responded with a bullet to the bad boy's heart.

❧

The legendary beauty and exotic dancer Mata Hari (born Margaretha Geertruida Zelle) was condemned to death in France in 1917 for the crime of espionage. Standing before the firing squad, her last request was for a small mirror. When the officer brought it to her, she daintily powdered her face and uttered her last words: *'Merci, monsieur.'*

Burmese kings seem to have been particularly unfortunate in the manner of their deaths. Three of them were trampled by elephants and one was killed by an enraged farmer after the king ate his cucumbers.

President Harry Truman left instructions indicating that he wanted to be buried in a casket of mulberry wood because, he said, 'I want to go through hell a-cracklin' and a-poppin'!'

In 1998, Nigerian dictator Sani Abacha arranged an orgy in his home with a couple of local prostitutes. He took some Viagra to get things started, and suffered a massive heart attack in the middle of the party.

Harold Holt, the prime minister of Australia in 1967, went for a swim in the waters near Melbourne one warm December day in 1967. 'I know this beach like the back of my hand,' he told a companion before he went into the water. He was never seen or heard from again.

❧

Dr. Eugene Shoemaker was the astronomer who codiscovered the Comet Shoemaker-Levy 9. He died in a car accident in 1997. His ashes were put on the space probe Lunar Prospector, and buried on the moon. He is the only person thus far to be laid to rest there.

❧

As the Pope lay dying of pneumonia in 1922, a New York City newspaper ran the headline POPE BENEDICT XV IS DEAD. When alerted of the error, the paper changed the headline in the next edition to read POPE HAS MIRACULOUS RECOVERY.

❧

The author Isak Dinesen, perhaps best known for her novel *Out of Africa* and whose real name was Karen von Blixen-Finecke, liked telling people that her husband Baron Bror Blixen-Finecke, who was also her second cousin, had contracted syphilis through one of his many extramarital dalliances and had given it to her in their first year of marriage. Far from considering the disease a source of shame, and despite the fact that she was convinced she would die of it, she rather liked having syphilis. In her view of the world, it was the disease of poets and heroes. It was also the disease of her father, who, upon learning that he had become infected, chose to kill himself rather than risk giving it to his wife.

The baron apparently recovered from his symptoms without medication. Dinesen, on the other hand consumed mercury and arsenic over a long period of time, which was the only known remedy in the early 1900s. Some medical scholars believe that it was the treatment, not the disease, which ultimately killed the brilliant author, who was twice nominated for a Nobel Prize.

❧

John Stonehouse, a member of the British Parliament, might have gotten away with faking his own death, but he was a little too conspicuous for his own good. He left a pile of clothes on a beach in Miami, Florida, leading the FBI and other American authorities to conclude he had committed suicide. This theory made sense because it was well known that Stonehouse had some serious financial difficulties back home. Stonehouse entered Australia on the stolen passport of a dead constituent and lived lavishly in Melbourne, posing as an English aristocrat. The actual identity of the aristocrat was another dead Londoner. Australian authorities became suspicious when Stonehouse tried to open a bank account with the £600,000 he had embezzled from a charity fund intended for victims of a hurricane in Bangladesh.

Stonehouse's wife was ecstatic upon hearing the news that her husband was still alive. That quickly changed when she arrived in Australia to find him living with his beautiful former secretary.

Stonehouse served only three of the seven years to which he was sentenced. He was given an early release because of heart problems. He did live another twelve years after his release, giving him plenty of time to write his autobiography, *Death of an Idealist*. He died of a heart attack in 1988.

❧

French grammarian, Dominique Bouhours, was a stickler to the end. His last words were, 'I am about to - or I am going to - die. Either expression is correct.'

❧

In the first century BC, King Fjölnir of Ynglingatal awoke in the night with the urgent need to relieve himself. He had passed out in his chambers after a long night of drinking and merriment. Still suffering the effects of his inebriation, he got lost on the way back to his quarters. He stumbled, fell into a barrel of beer, and drowned.

❧

The ancient Greek mathematician Archimedes was busy working out an equation, writing in the sand with a stick. The last words he ever spoke were 'Don't disturb my circles.' His fatal error was speaking those words to a Roman soldier.

❧

As Joan Crawford lay on her deathbed in 1977, her devoted housekeeper, assistant, and probably only true friend in the world, fell to her knees and began to pray out loud for the legendary actress. Crawford turned on her immediately. She propped herself up slightly and said, 'Damn it, don't you dare ask God to help me!' She was dead before her head hit the pillow.

❦

In the last moments of her life in 1964, Lady Astor, the first female member of the British Parliament, woke up from a light slumber only long enough to turn to the family members surrounding her deathbed and say, 'Am I dying? Or is this my birthday?'

❦

The daring French philosopher Voltaire frequently refuted the fiercely held religious beliefs of his times, despite the strict censorship laws of eighteenth-century France. When a priest at his deathbed asked him to renounce Satan, he replied, 'Now, now, dear man. This is not the time to be making enemies.'

❦

Helle Cristina Habsburg Windsor was considered by some to be an insufferable bore. She delighted especially in her claims of being a descendant of Spanish royalty. 'I was born on the steps of the throne!' she intoned a few times too many. 'So awkward for her mother,' noted her obituary writer.

❦

Holy Roman Emperor Frederick I, en route to the Third Crusade, stopped at the banks of the Saleph River for a cool drink of water. Stooped over, he suffered a heart attack. The weight of his armor pulled him face down into the riverbank. He drowned in water that was just a few inches deep.

King Louis II of Hungary also drowned in a shallow stream under the weight of his own armor. Louis, however, was not heading bravely into battle at the time. He was fleeing the Ottomans after leading his army to utter defeat in the Battle of Mohács in 1526.

∙❧∙

In the last years of his life, the great American poet Walt Whitman searched the depths of his soul for something glorious, a few brilliant and patriotic words to leave behind as his legacy for all of humanity. He gave up, finally, uttering only one word before dying: 'Shit.'

∙❧∙

The obscure and perplexing German philosopher Georg Hegel remained so to the very end. While on his deathbed in 1831, he said, 'Only one man ever understood me, and even he didn't understand me.'

∙❧∙

At the wake of legendary Hollywood film producer Samuel Goldwyn, his partner Louis B. Mayer remarked, 'The reason so many people showed up at the funeral was because they wanted to make sure he was dead.' On his own deathbed in 1957, Mayer's last words were, 'Nothing matters. Nothing matters.'

❦

William Henry Harrison, ninth president of the United States, refused to wear a coat to his inaugural speech, despite the fact that it was unusually cold in Washington D.C. that day in March 1841. Harrison's presidential address, the longest in American history, included the promise that he would not seek a second term in office. He kept his promise by dying of pneumonia one month later.

❦

Leon Trotsky, the Soviet revolutionary leader, was assassinated in 1940 while in exile in Mexico. It was not the first attempt on his life. His killer, a Spanish-born Soviet agent named Ramon Mercader, hit Trotsky over the head with an ice axe. Never one to go down without a fight, Trotsky tackled his assassin and fought him for several minutes before bodyguards entered the room. When the guards set upon Mercader, Trotsky shouted, 'Do not kill him! This man has a story to tell.' Trotsky then spat on Mercader and took a bite out of his leg. Trotsky died the following day at a local hospital.

❦

Emperor Louis the Pious, son of the great Charlemagne, King of the Francs, was literally scared to death when he experienced five minutes of total darkness during the lunar eclipse of AD 840.

4

DEATH'S LITTLE IRONIES

WE ARE BORN NAKED, WET, AND HUNGRY.
THEN THINGS GET WORSE.
Author unknown

ACCORDING TO THOSE *great academic thinkers who spend much of their lives figuring out such things, there are only three kinds of proper irony: tragic irony, Socratic irony and cosmic irony. Those great thinkers tend to look down their noses on a fourth kind: comic irony. Comic irony, they sniff, happens by accident, as when the unexpected outcome of a story 'startles' us into laughter. Not a single one of my college professors was funny and I'm sure that, by now, most of them are dead.*

Noted inventor Thomas Midgley, wheelchair-bound after having contracted polio in 1940, devised a mechanism comprised of ropes and pulleys that allowed him to hoist himself out of bed and get into his chair without assistance. He was found dead, suspended in midair, strangled in his own contraption.

The Russian physician, philosopher, economist, science fiction writer, and revolutionary, Alexander Bogdanov, believed that human rejuvenation was possible through blood transfusions from young donors. Very little was known about transfusions in the early 1900s, but this didn't stop Bogdanov from experimenting on himself. After eleven transfusions, he happily reported that his eyesight had improved and he was no longer going bald. Unfortunately, the youthful blood of his last donor also contained malaria and tuberculosis, which killed him.

James Douglas, the Earl of Morton, was executed in Scotland in 1581 for his role in the murder of the treacherous Henry Stuart, husband of Mary, Queen of Scots. Douglas was executed on The Maiden, a new and improved guillotine-like device that he himself had invented.

Thinning the Herd

❧

Famed baritone Leonard Warren suffered a stroke and collapsed on stage at the New York Metropolitan Opera in 1960. The opera was *La forza del destino* (the force of destiny). The last line he sang was, *'Morir? Tremenda cosa.'* ('To die? A wondrous thing.')

❧

Elisha Mitchell, geologist and explorer, slipped and died of a fall in 1857. He fell into Mitchell Falls in North Carolina, which he himself had named twenty-two years earlier. He is buried at the summit of Mount Mitchell.

❧

Stephen Davidson, a 35-year-old member of a cult known as the Barry Long Foundation, was found dead in 2005 in Butleigh Woods in Glastonbury, England. The coroner found particles of yew leaf in Davidson's throat, which is known to cause problems in the heart and lungs. Next to his body were a pile of sacred pebbles and healing crystals.

❧

While visiting her husband's grave in 2006, a Dutch woman suffered a fatal heart attack. She collapsed on the very plot where she was to be buried, under the headstone that was already inscribed with her name. She was found clutching a bag containing her will and explicit instructions for her funeral.

Tom Evans and Pete Ham, who were members of the popular band Badfinger, both committed suicide by hanging (Ham in 1975, and Evans in 1983). They were the authors of the song 'Without You,' which became a huge hit for Harry Nilsson, Mariah Carey, and Clay Aiken. The chorus of the song begins, 'I can't live, I can't live anymore.'

Brandon Lee was accidentally killed while filming the film *The Crow*. The scene went off as planned: a gun was fired, stage blood squirted, and Lee collapsed, mortally wounded. It wasn't until the end of the take that the crew realized Lee wasn't acting. A metal fragment that had become lodged in the prop pistol was discharged by the blanks when the gun was fired. That fragment fatally wounded the young actor.

Earl Metcalfe was a star in the early days of moviemaking. He enlisted with the famous 165th Infantry Division of the US army and was decorated five times for bravery during World War I. After the Armistice, he resumed his work as an actor, but never achieved the level of success he had attained prior to the war. His final film in 1928 was an aviation melodrama called *Air Mail Pilot*. The role inspired him to take flying lessons. He fell out of the training airplane and died.

꙳

Ettore and Rossana of Padua, Italy, had been married for many years. Ettore faithfully visited his wife in the hospital every day, where she had lain in a coma for several months in 2005 with little hope for recovery. Distraught over the loss of his longtime companion, Ettore committed suicide in the couple's home. Hours later, Rossana woke up.

꙳

Richard 'Doc' Brown held a master's degree in biomedical engineering, but was best known as a self-taught and well-respected roller-coaster safety expert. He often used himself as a guinea pig to test newly designed rides. In 2005, at the age of sixty-four, he died of head injuries when he slipped and fell in his own driveway.

꙳

Frank Silvera channeled a rugged handsomeness and commanding stage presence into a successful thirty-year acting career in stage, film, and television. In the years before his death, he appeared in many 1960s television dramas with such colorful titles as *Run for Your Life: The Shock of Recognition* and *The Rat Patrol: The Chain of Death Raid*. He accidentally electrocuted himself while trying to repair a garbage disposal.

Singer-songwriter Bobby Fuller had only one memorable hit in his short career, 'I Fought the Law (and the Law Won)' in 1965. A few weeks after the song hit the top of the charts, Fuller's body was found severely beaten and drenched in gasoline, propped up in the front seat of his mother's Oldsmobile. The Los Angeles coroner ruled the death a suicide.

British actor George Sanders won an Academy Award for his role as a sarcastic theatre critic in the film *All About Eve*. He also played the lead in the 1959 film *Death of a Scoundrel*, and a schoolteacher who takes his own life in *Village of the Damned*. According to the short note found in the room where he died, he killed himself because he was bored.

New York City doctor Nicholas Bartha would sooner die than let his money-grubbing, soon-to-be-ex-wife make off with half the value of their $6 million Upper East Side townhouse. And so it was. The building collapsed on top of him in the summer of 2006 when he tried to blow it up. The money-grubbing, no-longer-ex-wife, now-widow, of the doctor sold the vacant bit of prime real estate for $8.3 million a year later.

Thinning the Herd

In the sixth century BC, the philosopher Chilon of Sparta, who is credited for such words of wisdom as 'One must learn how to regulate one's own house well,' and 'Nothing in excess,' died as the result of an uncontrollable fit of laughter.

In February 2007, archaeologists in Italy discovered the remains of two people buried together more than five thousand years ago. The skeletal remains were entwined in a lovers' embrace. The archaeological dig took place in Mantua, just a few miles south of the hometown of Romeo and Juliet.

Singer Robert Palmer spent a lot of time and energy denying reports of his death in 1997 when a famous music critic by the same name died of liver disease at the age of fifty-two. Not long after the matter seemed finally to be settled, Robert Palmer the singer died of a heart attack at the age of fifty-four.

Jim Fixx, author of the 1970s best-seller *The Complete Book of Running*, died in 1980 of a heart attack while jogging.

Shortly after the publication of Charles Darwin's *The Origin of Species* in 1860, circus and sideshow mogul P. T. Barnum created a new sensation: Zip the Pinhead. Zip was billed as a wild man from Africa, Darwin's missing link between humans and primates. In actuality, Zip was just a guy from New Jersey named William Henry Johnson, who happened to have an oddly shaped head.

The hoax was only one of many in Barnum's big bag of lucrative tricks, but Zip became a shrewd businessman in his own right. After leaving Barnum's sideshow, he went on the road on his own. In a brilliant publicity stunt in 1925, he offered himself up as evidence during the so-called Scopes Monkey Trial, which challenged the teaching of Darwin's *The Origin of Species* in public schools.

Zip the Pinhead died at the age of sixty-six, a very happy and wealthy man. He spoke his last words to his sister: 'We sure fooled them, didn't we?'

Ten minutes into a 1996 performance of *The Makropulos Case* at the Metropolitan Opera in New York City, tenor Richard Versalle fell backward from a 10-foot ladder after singing the line, 'You can only live so long.'

Versalle fell flat on his back with his arms outstretched, hitting his head on the stage floor below. The fall alone would probably not have killed him. It was the massive heart attack that did him in.

Thinning the Herd

Summer Lynn Mau and Orem Kauvaka were among a group of fifteen young people who were setting up a roadside marker in Hawaii to serve as a memorial and a warning for reckless drivers. Two of their friends, Pepe Naupoto and Alitha Ah Nee, had been killed in a tragic accident the night before in June 2006. As the mourners stood there, another car plowed into the group and killed Summer and Orem. The following day, the remaining friends set up another marker.

Although Bobby Leach broke nearly every bone in his body, he survived a barrel ride over Niagara Falls in 1911. He made a full recovery and went on to travel the world, thrilling audiences with the tale of his adventure. While on tour, he suffered fatal injuries when he slipped on a fruit peel on a New Zealand street.

Yoshiuki Takada was an aerial performer with the Sankai Juku Dance Company of Toyko. In 1985, the troupe performed in Seattle, suspended over the side of the Mutual Life Building. Takada's rope broke and sent him hurtling to the pavement six stories below. The title of Takada's last performance was *The Dance of Birth and Death*.

Pedro Medina was a Cuban refugee convicted and sentenced to die for the stabbing death of a schoolteacher in 1982. If not for the grisly outcome of the execution, he would have quickly faded into obscurity, just another condemned prisoner.

It was the second time in seven years that Florida's electric chair had malfunctioned. Flames a foot high shot from the top of Medina's head. He did die, but not by electrocution; he was roasted alive in that chair.

The last words he spoke were, 'I am still innocent.'

5

SO SEXY IT HURTS

Life without sex might be safer, but it
would be unbearably dull.
Henry Louis Mencken

THE FIRST TIME *I let a boy kiss me, I was certain of three things:
that I was pregnant, that what I had done was written all over my
face for all the world to see, and that I was going to go to hell. Of course,
I wasn't pregnant, although hell is still a possibility (but that's a story for
another day). What was unbearably humiliating to me at that particular
moment in my young life was not the 'sin' itself, but the fact that other
people would know what I had done, and that such knowledge would
inevitably bring much pointing and snickering my way. I wonder if any
of the people in the following stories ever pondered a similar fate?*

Several popes throughout history were summarily ushered into the next life as a result of their naughty dalliances. Pope John VII was bludgeoned to death by the husband of his mistress when he caught them *in flagrante delicto*. John XIII met his end (so to speak) when a cuckolded husband rammed a poker up his bottom.

Other popes died a bit more privately. Pope Leo VII suffered a fatal heart attack during sex. Pope Paul II was said to have died while being sodomized by a page boy. More recently in history, the short-lived Pope John Paul I, known also as The Smiling Pope and who died just thirty-three days into his papacy, was allegedly so obsessed with pornography that he passed away while 'reviewing the literature.' (The Vatican is reputed to have one of the largest collections of pornography in the world.)

Nick Wallis of Oxford was rapidly succumbing to a debilitating neuromuscular disease and was spending his final days in a Catholic assisted-living facility. In 2006, he confided to Sister Frances Dominica, one of the nurses at the facility, that although he had lived a fairly happy life, his one great regret was that he had never had sex. Moved by the young man's plight, the good sister did the compassionate thing. She found him a prostitute on the Internet.

Thinning the Herd

❧

In the summer of 2001, Jean-Louis Toubon of Marseilles died while having sex with his girlfriend. He choked to death on her edible panties.

❧

In the summer of 2006, university students Jason Ackerman and Sara Rydman, seeking adventure and a little privacy, crawled inside a deflated helium balloon and got busy. They were found dead of helium poisoning.

❧

Kichizo Ishida frequently told his lover, Sada Abe, that he wished to die while having sex. So in 1936, she strangled him. She then cut off his penis and carried it in her kimono for several days before turning it over to the police. The penis was last seen at a department store exhibition in 1949.

❧

No one in Richard Pryor's family was particularly surprised when they heard that Richard's father had died while having sex in a brothel. Richard himself had been born in that brothel. His father was the pimp. His mother did double duty as a prostitute and book-keeper. Grandma was the house madam. Telling the story many years later and marveling over God's benevolence, Pryor said, 'My father came - and went - at the same time.'

In the summer of 2005, Kenneth Pinyan of Seattle, Washington died of a ruptured colon after he had anal intercourse with a horse. Law enforcement officials did not treat the case as a crime because bestiality was not illegal in Washington State at the time. Also, the horse was unharmed.

In 1899, the president of France, Félix Faure, died while receiving oral gratification from his mistress. When the woman became aware that the president had become 'unusually stiff,' she panicked and began to scream. The president's aides broke down the door when they heard the muffled cries. They found Faure seated on a sofa, with his mistress kneeling before him.

Separating the lovers turned out to be a rather complicated task. Faure died with the woman's long black hair clutched in his hands in a death grip. Further, the shock of realizing what had just happened to her caused the woman to suffer trauma-induced lockjaw. They did eventually free the hysterical woman from her lover's crotch, but doctors had to pry Faure's member from her clenched mouth.

The aides were later credited for having had the presence of mind to put their fallen leader in a more dignified pose before taking the woman to the hospital. The next day's newspapers showed a photograph of Faure lying in bed with his hands neatly folded over a crucifix.

❧

Grigory Rasputin, known also as 'The Mad Monk', was a trusted friend of the Romanovs, Russia's last royal family. Rasputin inspired more fear, awe, and envy, however, for the size of his penis than for his connections to the throne. Rasputin's foot-long member was festooned with an enormous wart, located in just such a position as to cause some of his lovers to lose consciousness.

After his death in 1916, Rasputin's penis became a collector's item. In 1995, someone claiming to be the rightful owner arranged to have it sold at auction at Christie's. The item was withdrawn, however, when investigators discovered that it was a sea cucumber, not a penis. The genuine article is currently on display at the Erotic Museum in St. Petersburg, which also operates as a prostate clinic under the direction of Dr. Igor Knyazkin.

Another famously deceased penis was the one once attached to Napoleon Bonaparte. It was severed at his autopsy, then stolen shortly thereafter. It resurfaced some years later and was purchased by an American urologist for $40,000 in 1977. In comparing this specimen to Rasputin's, Dr. Knyazkin described Napoleon's little friend as, 'but a small pod.'

❧

Anthony Casey fell sixty feet from a balcony to his death during a drug-fueled gay orgy in London in 2006, in an apartment owned by Count Gottfried von Bismarck. The coroner listed the cause of death as 'misadventure.'

In 1975, American cartoonist Vaughn Bodé accidentally suffocated while having sex with himself. Some reports of his death indicate that he was riding a motorcycle at the time.

Silent film star Ramon Novarro was one of the most handsome and admired actors of his time. He did make it into the talkies, but his star quickly waned and he fell into relative obscurity during his final years. On Halloween night in 1968, two assailants broke into his home and bludgeoned him to death with one of Novarro's most cherished possessions: an art deco dildo given to him by his friend, Rudolph Valentino.

The ancient custom of *minghun* is still alive and well in certain remote regions of China. It involves burying a 'ghost bride' (a recently deceased woman) with a dead bachelor, so that he won't be lonely in the afterlife.

The enterprising pimping team of Yang Dongyan and Liu Shenghai figured out that they could get more money for a dead woman than a live prostitute, so they went into business with an undertaker. In 2006, Chinese police arrested all three men for murdering young women for the purpose of selling them as ghost brides.

⚜

Brocket Hall in Hertfordshire is rife with stories of the sexual exploits of its past residents. Lady Caroline Lamb once arranged herself inside a large soup tureen and had the servants serve her naked to her lover, Lord Byron. The elderly yet spry prime minister Lord Palmerston died happily on his own billiard table after helping himself to a young parlor maid. Brocket Hall is now a successful conference center, very popular with the corporate folk.

⚜

Silent film star Virginia Rappe died of massive internal injuries after having sex with the 300-pound comic actor Roscoe 'Fatty' Arbuckle. After three sensational trials, Fatty was cleared of any wrongdoing, but he never worked in Hollywood again. He just wasn't so funny after that.

⚜

Mervin Touchet, second Earl of Castlehaven, was executed in 1631 on two counts of sodomy and one of abetting rape. If he had been allowed to plead innocent because he was clergy, he might have been exonerated, as many other clerics of the day had been lucky enough to do. Instead, he got the guillotine.

❧

In 2004, a 68-year-old mother from Seville, Spain, was horrified to find her 45-year-old bachelor son having sex with a blow-up doll. She destroyed the offensive object by popping it with a pin. The man responded by stabbing his mother sixty-one times.

❧

Zhou Jingzhi thought he had come up with a uniquely satisfying way of mending his broken heart and restoring his honor as a man: he forcibly tattooed insults on the bodies of women who had rejected him as a lover. The Chinese government was not pleased. Zhou Jingzhi was sentenced to death for his crime.

❧

Legendary womanizer Giacomo Casanova once boasted of having bested the ultimate jealous husband - God himself - when a gorgeous yet duplicitous nun passed him a note one day and invited him into her bed. It was an invitation extended many times by the naughty nun, and accepted just as often by the lascivious Casanova.

Casanova died in the Castle of Dux in Bohemia in 1798, a lonely old man. He was despised and shunned by nearly everyone, including the servants. His last words, spoken to Prince de Ligne, were as ironic as they were magnificently self-deceiving: 'I have lived as a philosopher, and die as a Christian.'

❧

The body of a man clad in a kinky black leather mask and decked out head to toe in sadomasochistic gear was found hanging from a chain-link fence in Lower Manhattan in September 2006. Untold numbers of New Yorkers walked by and ignored him, assuming the corpse was just an early Halloween display.

❧

A 65-year-old German retiree living on the Costa del Sol was the proud inventor of a homemade sex toy. He rigged a voltmeter in such a way that he could apply the electrodes to his genitalia to give himself an extra little buzz. In 2003, he popped a porn tape into the VCR and flipped the switch on his new toy. He was found some time later, still wired, dead of a heart attack.

❧

Albert Dekker, star of the 1940 film *Dr. Cyclops,* was found hanging from a shower curtain rod, with dirty hypodermic needles in each arm, wearing women's lingerie, and obscenities written in lipstick all over his body. Not quite sure what to make of the scene, officials ruled that the death of the 62-year-old actor was 'accidental suicide' - a series of autoerotic escapades gone slightly haywire.

An unidentified couple in Bucharest was found dead, post-coitus, in their car. They had, apparently, forgotten the most important safety rule for having sex in the backseat of a car: either turn off the ignition or open the garage door.

6

RAMPAGE OF ANGELS

EVERY NORMAL MAN MUST BE TEMPTED AT TIMES
TO SPIT UPON HIS HANDS, HOIST THE BLACK FLAG,
AND BEGIN SLITTING THROATS.

Lucanus (AD 39–65)

ANGRY, OUT-OF-CONTROL, *raging people scare me. I have a very long fuse, myself. Eventually, of course, it runs out, but it can take years before I realize that something is really bothering me. Would that we all could always find a few more inches of fuse. But of course, some of us don't.*

On a rural road in the mountain region of Pantelhó, Mexico, in 2006, an argument broke out between two families over who was responsible for repairing a pothole. The dispute ended in gunfire, with four people dead, three others injured, and the pothole still unrepaired.

In 1905, in a rage over not being able to remember the combination code to the safe in his office, Jack Daniel, founder of the famous Tennessee whiskey distillery, kicked the safe and broke his toe. He died of blood poisoning a few days later.

Carl Panzram of Minnesota began his career as a serial killer at the age of eight. Later in life he added 'nomad' to his list of skills, and slaughtered people on nearly every continent on the planet. While in Africa, he once killed six men in a single day and fed their bodies to the crocodiles. He was finally captured and sentenced to death by hanging in 1930. On the day of his execution, Panzram ran gleefully up the steps of the Leavenworth Penitentiary's gallows, spat in his executioner's face, and yelled, 'Hurry up, you bastard! I could've killed ten men while you're fooling around here!'

Thinning the Herd

Crusty old Captain Ford was not particularly fond of surprises. He returned to his New Hampshire home after a long voyage at sea in 1741, and promptly murdered his beautiful young wife Elizabeth. The captain had not seen Elizabeth in nearly a year, but there she was, nursing a baby.

꒰ꙮ꒱

Suresh Kumar, a 25-year-old tailor from Bangalore doused himself in gasoline and set himself on fire in protest against the 1996 Miss World beauty pageant. Before lighting the match, Kumar shouted slogans criticizing the pageant's exploitation of women. His last words were reportedly, 'Water! Water! Water!'

꒰ꙮ꒱

Amish teenager Danny Crawford was out having a little old-fashioned fun with some friends in December 2006. They were tossing tomatoes at passing cars. Danny was shot to death by an irate motorist who didn't think it was that funny.

꒰ꙮ꒱

While attending a wedding in Cancún, Mexico, in 2007, a British couple got into a bit of a spat on the balcony of their fourteenth-floor luxury hotel room. Adrian Fletcher and his girlfriend Lisa Miller began arguing after an all-night drinking session in the hotel lobby. At one point, Fletcher picked up his girlfriend and threw her off the balcony, but he fell with her. Fortunately, they both landed on the balcony of the floor just below them. When hotel security guards burst onto the scene, Fletcher spread his arms like some kind of giant bird, smiled, and took a dive over the railing, aiming for the swimming pool below. Even if he had hit the water, it is unlikely that he would have survived the fall. As it happened, he landed on the concrete deck.

🐁

Ryuji Sakamoto had held his tongue for as long as he could. He simply could not fathom why his friend Takayuki Niimi persisted in his refusal to address Mr. Sakamoto using the respectful honorific 'san' after his first name. Then one day in 2002, he snapped. He punched Niimi in the face several times, knocked him to the floor, and stabbed him in the head with his umbrella. Interestingly, Niimi was the second person to be stabbed in the head with an umbrella in Japan that month.

🐁

Immigration lawyer Richard Baumhammers went on a homicidal rampage in his suburban Pennsylvania neighborhood in April of 2000. Baumhammers drove his Jeep from house to house, killing five people he had singled out for their race or ethnicity. His attorney explained that the rampage was merely an outward expression of Baumhammers's belief that he was being watched by the FBI, that his maid was a spy, and that his skin was falling off.

In January 2007, a man from the Karelia region of Russia stabbed and bludgeoned his 81-year-old grandmother to death when they could not agree on what program to watch on television. In court, the man's lawyer said his client was drunk at the time and could not remember exactly what it was he had wanted to watch.

❧

To better exert their authority, or perhaps for their own protection, health officials in China often travel in very large groups. In July 2001, fifty meat inspectors paid a visit to Guan Jiadong's butcher shop. Citing serious health hazards, they began to confiscate the meat. Guan Jiadong grabbed a bunch of his knives, hopped on his motorbike, and plowed straight into the group. He hacked four of the inspectors to death right where they stood. He also managed to carve a few large chunks out of three other men before he was finally subdued.

❧

A 59-year-old Dutch man was fed up with the way the Philips electronics company was peddling its wide-screen television sets, which he considered to be inferior in quality. So he went to the Rembrandt Tower in downtown Amsterdam and took eighteen employees hostage at gunpoint. What he had not realized was that Philips had moved to the building next door the year before, in 2001. Seven hours into the siege, the hostage-taker went into the men's room and shot himself in the head. The first bullet didn't kill him, so he shot himself again. Police later described the man as 'confused.'

🐂

Marc Lépine will probably go down in history as Canada's worst mass murderer. He went on a shooting spree in 1989 at a technical college in Montreal, shouting, 'I hate feminists!' He killed fourteen women before turning the gun on himself. The dealer who sold Lépine the gun later said of the disturbed young man, 'He didn't appear any crazier than anybody else.'

🐂

A 2006 marital dispute in Hamilton Heights, New York turned tragic when Donna Cobbs beat her husband Kevin with a ceramic elephant. When he collapsed, Donna tried to resuscitate him by giving him CPR. Kevin died at Harlem Hospital, where Donna worked as a nurse.

🐂

Lloyd Robert Jeffress took an AK-47 and a sawed-off .22-caliber rifle into a Benedictine monastery in rural Missouri and shot the priest who greeted him at the door. He also shot a Brother who was tending the garden. Monks all over the monastery ran away in terror and hid in their rooms. Jeffress wandered the halls of the monastery's business offices and shot a few more people, and then went to sit in the chapel for a while. The last shot he fired was into his own head. Jeffress's ex-wife later told police that he'd been very angry over their divorce. Their marriage had ended forty-three years earlier.

❧

No one felt particularly compelled to render aid to suspected serial killer Moninder Singh Pandher, not even his own attorneys. At Pandher's arraignment in January 2007, lawyers from both sides of the table, court officers, and even the judge dragged Pandher into the streets and kicked him all the way to the district court police station. They punched him, kneed him in the groin, and pulled the hairs out of his moustache. They also yanked his pants off. Some lawyers stood on top of parked cars and led the frenzied crowds of spectators in chanting, 'Kill the cannibal!' Pandher, who was charged with the gruesome murders of at least twenty-one people, was turned in by his own servant, a man curiously named Surendra.

❧

In 1827, Joseph Smith found a holy book on a hill near his home in Palmyra, New York, and founded the Mormon religion. He managed to organize a rather large group of followers over the coming years, but learned soon enough that great power often breeds great enemies. By the spring of 1844, a number of prominent Mormons in Illinois, where Smith was then living, set out to expose Smith as a fraud based on rumors of polygamy, strange sexual liaisons, and other unorthodox practices. Smith responded by ordering the destruction of the free press. Satisfied that Smith had sealed his own fate and proven himself to be a theocratic tyrant, the dissidents murdered him in his own jail cell, where Smith had hoped to hide from the angry mob until the kerfuffle blew over. Brigham Young gathered up the remaining followers and fled Illinois. They didn't stop until they got to Utah.

ॐ

A protest over the food on board the RMS *Queen Mary* during World War II escalated into a riot. American troops being transported across the Atlantic had become increasingly dissatisfied with the cook's disgusting concoctions, which became less edible with each passing day. Unable to take it anymore, the rioters beat the man senseless, stuffed him into his own oven, and baked him to death.

ॐ

Barbara Graham and two accomplices were convicted of beating and strangling a handicapped widow in Burbank, California in 1955. Graham was sentenced to die in the gas chamber at the San Quentin penitentiary. As the executioner escorted her into the chamber, he said, 'Now take a deep breath and it won't bother you.' Barbara looked at him sideways and replied, 'How in the hell would you know?!'

꧁

A 57-year-old Bulgarian woman in the last stages of terminal cancer was granted a 'mercy release' from prison. She had been serving time for killing her own son with a garden hoe in 2005 while he was sleeping. As soon as she got home, she stabbed her husband in the throat. He died. The woman was immediately taken back into custody, but promised that, if released, she would kill her other son.

꧁

James French was found guilty of killing a motorist in 1958 and was sentenced to life in prison. Disappointed that he was not to be executed, and unable to kill himself despite several tries, French took another approach: he strangled his cellmate to death. At last, French got his wish. Strapped into Oklahoma's electric chair in 1966, he turned to witnesses and reporters and said, 'How's this for tomorrow's headline? FRENCH FRIES!'

꧁

Clara Harris of Texas was forced to recant her initial claim that the death of her husband was an accident. She had been caught on tape in 2002 behind the wheel of her Mercedes-Benz, running him over - and over and over - in the parking lot of a Houston hotel. Clara had followed her husband and his mistress into the lobby of the hotel, where all three were promptly thrown out by guards when the loud confrontation between the wife, the husband and his lover turned into a fistfight. All of this occurred in the very hotel in which Mr. and Mrs. Harris had celebrated their wedding reception a decade earlier.

✌

The prescription sleep aid Halcion was banned in the United States and Britain in the early 1990s after numerous reports of adverse side effects, including mild amnesia and disorientation. The ban came a little too late for Mildred Coates. The 83-year-old Iowa woman was found by police, stretched out on her bed, clutching a cheery birthday card in her left hand and with her brains splattered across her pillow. Her daughter, 63-year-old insomniac Ilo Grundberg, had no clear recollection of having shot her mother nine times in the head.

✦

7

IT SEEMED LIKE A GOOD IDEA AT THE TIME

In view of the fact that God limited the intelligence of man,
it seems unfair that he did not also limit his stupidity.
Konrad Adenauer (1876–1967)

AT ANY GIVEN *moment in time, somebody has to be the stupidest
person in the world. I believe wholeheartedly that that's a provable
mathematical fact. We all get a turn at some point in our lives.
Most of us will live to pass the baton on to the next hapless
moron-du-jour. Some of us, alas, do not.*

Michael Warner of Texas missed drinking since contracting a particularly nasty throat ailment. In the spring of 2005, he and his wife, Tammy, devised a clever workaround: Tammy gave her husband a wine enema. It turned out to be an ingenious way of ingesting alcohol but, unfortunately, it killed him.

An old World War II bomb blew up and killed a fisherman off the coast of Tirana, Albania in July of 1996. The man had intended to detonate the bomb in the ocean to facilitate catching massive amounts of fish at once. Although it is illegal in Albania to kill fish with explosives, many fishermen continue to make use of the numerous old bombs that still litter the coast. Dead and dismembered fishermen are also numerous in this part of the world.

Charles G. Stephens thought he had figured out why so many people had killed themselves going over Niagara Falls in a barrel: they didn't use a counterweight. So in the summer of 1920, Charles outfitted his wooden barrel with an anvil, got inside, and strapped himself in. The only part of Charles G. Stevens that was ever found was his right arm, still inside the barrel.

Thinning the Herd

In 1753, Professor Georg Richmann of St. Petersburg, Russia, wanted to test the effects of lightning during a thunderstorm. He attached a wire to the top of his house and connected it to a device made up of an insulated rod and an iron bar suspended above a bowl filled with water and brass filings. As Richmann and his assistant observed the approach of a distant storm, a ball of lightning suddenly bounced off the rod and smacked Richmann on the forehead. Richmann's shoes were blown apart, his clothes were singed, the doorframe was split open, and the door was torn off its hinges. Richmann looked remarkably peaceful despite the fact that he was lying flat on his back, quite dead. His wife saw him and thought he was napping, so she left him there. His assistant woke up after a brief moment of unconsciousness. Except for a few scattered pellets, the contraption was utterly undisturbed.

The widow of a US marine thought she had planned the perfect murder. Cynthia Sommer slowly poisoned her husband to collect $250,000 in veterans' benefits. She used the money for better clothes, parties, and a boob job.

In an effort to simultaneously cover her tracks and appear noble in her new role as the widow of a war hero, she donated Todd Sommer's organs to a local hospital upon his death in February 2002. She had the rest of him cremated. Lab tests on the donated organs revealed hundreds of times the normal level of arsenic in his liver and kidneys. Cynthia was, as they say, busted.

In January 2006, David Galvan and his uncle Rafael Vargas were having a good time drinking in their home in Barranquilla, Colombia. At some point during the evening, Galvan was overcome by a terrible bout of the hiccups. Vargas knew the perfect cure for this malady: He pointed a gun at his nephew. The hiccups stopped immediately after the gun went off. Horrified over the accidental killing, Vargas then turned the gun on himself.

A 63-year-old German retiree ran a high-voltage cable into his vegetable patch to wipe out the moles in his garden in 2007. The voltage was enough to run a cement mixer. The man electrocuted himself on the first try. The moles survived.

Christian Ponce became yet one more killer in a long line of elusive criminals who were captured for reasons that had nothing to do with their crimes. Ponce was wanted in Ecuador in connection with the 1999 assassination of a former presidential candidate and his bodyguard. Seven years later, while driving along a country road outside Buffalo, New York, he was stopped for driving without a seat belt.

Other criminals who wished they had taken a bus more often include serial killers Ted Bundy, David 'Son of Sam' Berkowitz, and Henry Lee Lucas.

In August 2006, the owner of a tree service in Pleasant Prairie, Wisconsin was sucked into his own wood chipper and spat out the other end in little bitty pieces. The wood chipper had become clogged with a loose piece of wood, so he kicked it a few times to dislodge it. The chipper roared back to life. The gardener did not.

❧

At a Christmas party in Aurora, Colorado in 2000, Manuel Dominguez-Quintero dared his friend to shoot a plastic drinking cup off his head with a .25-caliber semiautomatic pistol. William Tell he was not. The bullet went directly into Manuel's head. The plastic cup was untouched.

❧

Stuntman A. J. Bakunas made it into the *Guinness Book of World Records* for performing the highest film stunt jump without a parachute. During the filming of the 1997 film *Steel*, he successfully performed a fall from the ninth floor of a construction site in Lexington, Kentucky. When he learned that Dar Robinson, another stuntman, had broken his record high-fall, Bakunas repeated the stunt, but this time from the top of the 300-foot construction site. Bakunas executed the jump expertly, but the air bag he landed on exploded. Bakunas died on impact.

Derek Kieper, an intensely vocal opponent of the seat-belt laws he considered 'intrusions on civil liberties and expensive to enforce,' died in 2004 when he was ejected from a Ford Explorer that skidded off an icy section of Interstate 80 in Nebraska. The driver and two other passengers, who were wearing seat belts, survived.

In July 1993, Toronto attorney Gary Hoy was demonstrating the strength of the windows in the climate-controlled high-rise building where he worked. He had previously tested the glass, and was now proving to his colleagues that the window could not be forced open in any way. He ran toward the window, hit it with his shoulder, and plunged twenty-four stories to his death.

In July 1989, five men from the same farming family died after falling into a manure pit. The first man to enter the pit was quickly overcome by toxic gases and lost consciousness. The others followed one at a time, each attempting to save the one who had gone in before him. A carpet installer working at the farmhouse also tried to help, but was pulled out by his assistant. The five men were finally dragged out of the pit by a local farm equipment salesman. He and two of his employees were the only ones to attempt the rescue using the rope that was hanging in the barn near the manure pit.

Thinning the Herd

❧

A helicopter carrying a nuclear research scientist, the deputy director of a radiation laboratory, and other luminaries went down in shallow water in California in 1958. The chopper landed on its side, with the main cabin door underwater. Some of the people on board were able to escape through the windows on the exposed side. With the cabin rapidly filling with water, one of the bright minds still inside the helicopter decided to pull the cord that inflated a twenty-man life raft. The raft immediately blocked the few remaining exits. All of the passengers had survived the crash, but the ones trapped inside the chopper drowned.

❧

In the mid-1980s, Vladmir Boronov, a blacksmith from Irkutsk, Russia found an old artillery shell left over from the war, and used it as an anvil for more than ten years. He was blown to bits one day when his hammer hit the shell in just the right place.

❧

In 2001, Caleb Rebh's Halloween job was to jump out of the woods and scare people when they rode by on the back of a hay truck. Certain he could do better, he climbed up a tree and took the place of a hanging skeleton that was rigged to drop down when the caravan passed by. Caleb carefully arranged the ropes to make sure his feet touched the ground so he wouldn't accidentally hang himself. When the caravan approached, he leapt from the tree. The branch whipped back and choked him to death anyway.

❧

In 2002, Chante Mallard, a nurse's aide from Fort Worth, Texas hit a homeless man with her car, then drove home with him still stuck to her windshield. When she was arrested, she denied that she had ignored the man's cries for help for three days, and let him bleed to death in her garage. However, she did not dispute the fact that her boyfriend had dumped the man's body in a nearby park.

❧

After having a bit too much to drink one night in 2005, a 29-year-old woman from Belgium took a shortcut through a cemetery on her way home from the bar. At some point in the journey, she felt she could no longer 'hold it,' so she crouched between two graves and relieved herself. One of the headstones toppled over and crushed her to death.

❧

The line that separates the virtual world and the one the rest of us inhabit sometimes becomes a little blurry for certain dedicated online gamers. In January 2005, Xiao Yi jumped from the top of a twenty-four-story building in China, believing he would end up in cyberspace with his 'real friends,' all of whom were characters in his Internet role-playing game.

A surgeon and a university professor from Uzbekistan were also a husband-and-wife team of part-time travel agents. The two were arrested in 2001 on charges that they were killing off customers with the intention of selling their organs to brokers in Russia. Authorities found six bodies, dozens of passports, and about $40,000 in US currency in the couple's home.

At a 2002 gathering of friends one night in Daventry, Northamptonshire Kevin Barnes fashioned a make-believe pipe bomb from a firecracker. He put the improbable device in his mouth, flicked a lighter, and chuckled, 'Tick, tick, boom!' The fuse flickered and fizzled. Then the firecracker exploded. Barnes died of his self-inflicted head injuries.

The English explorer John Davis discovered the Falkland Islands off the coast of Antarctica in 1592. The seventy-six-man crew needed to ensure that they would have enough food in their stores to complete the journey home without starving, so they slaughtered 14,000 penguins. As soon as the ship reached the tropics, every bit of the meat spoiled. Of the original seventy-six-man crew, only sixteen returned alive.

In 1930s New York, five bar buddies came up with the perfect get-rich-quick scheme: Take out a life insurance policy on a homeless man, kill him, and collect the benefits. Michael Malloy, the lucky bum, was the perfect foil - barely lucid, always drunk, and hardly able to remain upright even on his best days. The Murder Trust, as they would be known, obtained three policies totaling less than $1,800, with a double-indemnity clause if Malloy died accidentally.

One of the members of the Trust owned a bar. The men decided that the least-conspicuous way to kill Malloy was to help him finish drinking himself to death. Malloy came back night after night, no worse for the wear, so the bartender started serving him shots of antifreeze. That had no less an adverse effect on him than whiskey. They tried turpentine, horse liniment, and rat poison. Malloy couldn't tell the difference between any of those either, and continued to show up every night for his free drinks. He even loved the sandwiches made of spoiled sardines, carpet tacks, and tin can shavings he was served with his turpentine one night.

Frustrated and desperate, the gang finally took Malloy to a deserted intersection in the Bronx. After getting him drunk on antifreeze, they ran him over with a car a couple of times. Triumph at last.

Two weeks later, Malloy walked into the bar and apologized for his absence. He had recently had to spend some time in the hospital, he told them.

All out of fresh ideas for disposing of Malloy in any subtle way, the Trust took him upstairs to the bartender's room. They

Thinning the Herd

ran a hose from the gas stove to Malloy's mouth and waited for him to turn purple. The next morning, finally, Malloy was dead.

In the end, the Murder Trust was its own nemesis. Suspicious of one another, they began talking to people outside the group. They were eventually caught and stood trial. All five went to prison. Four of them got the electric chair.

❧

In what is surely the most dangerous and idiotic schoolyard game ever devised by children, 32-year-old Janet Rudd choked to death on a mouthful of marshmallows at the 2006 Western Ontario fair. The winner of the game is the person who can stuff the most marshmallows in his or her mouth without swallowing them, and still be able to say 'Chubby Bunny.' The losers are usually the people who cut off their own air supply with an immovable gob of marshmallow, as Janet Rudd did.

❧

In his desire to bring China to greater glory and perhaps become an aeronautical pioneer in the process, a minor officer in the fourteenth century's Ming Dynasty named Wan Hu tried to launch himself into outer space. He tied a rocket to a chair, strapped himself in, and lit the fuse. The contraption exploded, sending him far outward, but not very far upward.

❧

Eri van den Biggelaar had been a teacher for forty years when she was diagnosed with terminal cancer in February 2007. Beloved by faculty and students alike, she was offered a parting gift: the students in shop class built her a casket. While waiting for Ms. van den Biggelaar to die, they kept it in an empty classroom. The younger schoolchildren pretended the coffin was a submarine and used it during playtime.

❧

In 1998, Hugo Weicht threw a giant party to mark his twentieth anniversary as a master brewer. In the middle of the celebration, Weicht took a dive into a giant vat of beer. Friends and relatives at the party were unable to pull him out. He drowned in his own brew.

❧

Dominga Atherton and her daughter Gertrude were not very nice people. They frequently humiliated George, Gertrude's husband in public, referring to him as 'the weaker sex.' One day in 1887, George received an invitation to visit friends in Chile. He jumped at the chance to escape the torments of his contemptuous wife and mother-in-law. Sadly, poor hapless George suffered kidney failure on board the ship long before reaching Chile. Unsure of what else to do, the captain stored George in a barrel of rum to preserve him, then transferred him, barrel and all, to another ship heading back home to San Francisco.

As luck would have it, the pickled George arrived on Gertrude's doorstep several days before the note the captain had written explaining what had happened. Dominga and Gertrude were soon forced to leave the lavish residence, half crazy and convinced the house was haunted by George's ghost.

❧

In 1925, experienced cave explorer Floyd Collins went looking for a new entrance from Crystal Cave in Kentucky to the nearby Mammoth Cave. A rock fell on him, trapping him inside for more than two weeks. When his body was finally recovered, Floyd was given a decent burial in the family plot. The incident was such a sensation, however, that his family exhumed the body and placed it in a glass casket at the entrance to the cave, making it one of the most ghoulish and lucrative tourist attractions in 1920s America. All went well until someone stole the corpse. The body was later returned, but, strangely, Floyd's left leg was missing. It was never found.

❧

Over the years, Mrs. Purcell's patience wore rather thin with regard to her brilliant husband, English composer Henry Purcell. Annoyed that he had not yet arrived from the theater hours after the performance had ended, she locked him out of the house to teach him a lesson. Purcell died of exposure. He is buried in the floor of Westminster Abbey, next to the church's massive pipe organ.

A group of coworkers in India were engaged in a little harmless horseplay one fine day, as was their habit. As a joke, one of them grabbed an air-pump hose and released a blast of compressed air right between the back pockets of his buddy's pants, inadvertently blowing up his intestines.

Henry David Thoreau, American author and transcendentalist best known for his reflections on living simply and in harmony with nature, contracted tuberculosis in his late teens in 1835. He suffered the effects of this disease on and off for nearly thirty years. His fatal mistake may have been deciding to go outside late one rainy night to count the rings on a tree stump. He developed bronchitis and uttered these final, immortal words: 'Moose. Indian.'

The HMS *Curacao* was one of several smaller ships escorting the massive *Queen Mary* luxury liner in the North Atlantic during World War II. The spunky little *Curacao* cut in front of the 81,000-ton *Queen Mary* and was sliced right through the middle. Too bad it was wartime, too. Otherwise, the *Queen Mary* might have been allowed to stop and save some of the 439 men that were hurled into the water. Only 101 of them survived.

✿

Frustrated and angry over not being able to pay his real estate taxes, a 56-year-old Slovakian man identified only as Frantisek took a homemade guillotine to the local tax office in 2002 and set about the task of chopping off his own head. The device did not decapitate him, but it mangled him so badly that he died anyway.

✿

For some musicians, the bathroom is the most dangerous place in the world. Keith Relf of The Yardbirds was electrocuted in his London home while tuning his guitar in 1976; he was taking a bath at the time. Claude François, a French pop singer, electrocuted himself in 1978 when he tried to fix a broken lightbulb while standing in his bathtub.

✿

Ants have been used for centuries in the art and science of Chinese medicine. A Beijing businessman named Wang Zhendong figured out how to make a lucrative business from this bit of knowledge, selling ant farms to practitioners and medical suppliers and promising a 60 percent return on their investment. There were only two small problems: the farms failed to produce any ants, and Wang sold the $25 kits for $1,300 apiece. Wang was sentenced to death in 2007 for swindling $385 million from his customers.

Phyllis Parker, whose father owned the Vealtown Tavern during the American Revolutionary War, fell in love with Dr. Bynam, a tenant at the inn. Shortly after they were married, Bynam was exposed as a British spy and was hanged for treason. General Anthony Wayne had his corpse delivered in a box to the inn. Not knowing what was inside, Phyllis opened the crate and was greeted by the bug-eyed corpse of her husband. She never recovered from the fright.

CHAPTER

8

PLAY BALL!

NOBODY IN FOOTBALL SHOULD BE CALLED A GENIUS.
A GENIUS IS A GUY LIKE NORMAN EINSTEIN.
Joe Theismann

GUTS. PASSION. SKILL. *Luck. Strength. Fearlessness. It takes
all of these things to achieve a spectacularly stupid death. It is a
mistake, however, to assume that all jocks are stupid and therefore,
more likely than the rest of us to die weirdly. In this respect,
their fans can be equally stupid.*

The ancient Greek athlete Arrichion was a two-time champion of a particularly violent Olympic event called *pakration*, a wrestling-choking-finger-breaking sort of game. In his third bid for the crown in 564 BC, Arrichion's opponent jumped on his back and tried to strangle him from behind (a perfectly legal move in those days). Arrichion countered the attack by wrenching his upper body with such enormous speed and force that his opponent flew off his back and fell to the ground. The man broke his ankle, and Arrichion broke his own neck. The judges proclaimed Arrichion the winner before realizing the great athlete was dead. They placed the laurel crown on his head anyway.

❧

Mexican female wrestler Juana Barraza, known professionally as 'The Silent One,' shared a house with her mother. Despite these living arrangements, the two women had not spoken to each other in many years. Rather than allow the silence and strife to embitter her personal life, Barraza successfully channeled her rage into her on-stage persona.

Barraza was arrested in Mexico City in 2006 and identified as the vicious serial killer *Mataviejitas* (Killer of Little Old Ladies). She was accused of strangling as many as thirty elderly women. Barraza later told police that the victims reminded her of her mother.

Thinning the Herd

❧

A ferryboat hit a well-lit reef in September 2000 and sank off the coast of Paros, Greece. At least ninety people on board were killed. The crew had put the boat on autopilot so they could watch a football match.

❧

A Boston woman in a rowdy crowd celebrating the Red Sox's defeat of the New York Yankees in the 2004 American League Championship Series was killed when a policeman fired a pepper-spray pellet gun. Ordinarily, these pellets are non-lethal, but this one hit Victoria Snelgrove in the eyeball. The cop later said he was actually aiming at some other unruly fan.

❧

For centuries, many Middle Eastern countries have welcomed the arrival of spring with elaborately staged kite festivals. In each village, virtually every inhabitant participates in the colorful ritual. Skillful kite fliers prepare spools of string covered with shards of glass, razors, and wire, and engage in a sort of duel. The idea is to crisscross kite strings until the opponents' kites are cut loose and sent billowing into the stratosphere or plummeting back to earth.

In 2005, Pakistan banned the annual festival after nineteen people were killed. One man was decapitated by a razor-sharp kite string, and over two hundred others were injured.

＊

Former French rugby captain Marc Cecillon sought solace in a bottle after his retirement from professional sports. While attending a large party in 2004, he slapped a woman in the face. The hosts asked Cecillon to leave. When Cecillon's wife refused to go with him, he left her there. He returned to the party a short time later with his revolver and shot her. In court, Cecillon testified that this was all a misunderstanding. He had only meant to convince his wife that he was serious about them leaving the party together.

＊

Despite the fact that Thailand has never competed in a soccer World Cup match, two very enthusiastic Thai men cheered loudly for the Italian team while watching the 2006 games on a television in a restaurant in Bangkok. One of the restaurant patrons, unappreciative of the noise, asked the men to please quiet down. When they refused, the diner shot them both at point-blank range.

＊

Devan Young, a 29-year-old night maintenance worker from Wichita, Kansas was found dead by his coworkers early one morning in 2003. He was trapped in the pin-resetting machine in the bowling alley where he worked the night shift.

❧

Albert Short was an English hot-air balloon enthusiast and aircraft designer in the 1920s and 1930s. After safely landing one of his seaplanes, he dropped dead of a heart attack right in his own cockpit.

❧

Vladimir Smirnov, a champion fencer from the Soviet Union, suffered a fatal injury before a live audience during the 1982 Olympics. His opponent's foil pierced Smirnov's mask, entered his eyeball, and lanced his brain. Smirnov died nine days later.

❧

In 1983, professional diver Sergei Chalibashvili attempted the Dive of Death - a three-and-a-half reverse somersault in the tuck position. He jumped up, hit the board with his head, tumbled through the air several times, crashed into the water, and sank to the bottom of the pool. He was most likely dead long before he hit the water.

❧

Danish cyclist Knut Jensen died during the 1960 Rome Olympics. He collapsed of sunstroke in the middle of the race. Blood tests later revealed the presence of amphetamines and a metabolism booster. He might have survived either one of these conditions but he seriously injured himself when he landed on his head.

A nineteen-year-old man named Jeff Bailey died of a heart attack after scoring 16,660 on Berzerk, a popular video arcade game of the early 1980s. This was the first known instance of dying - for real - while playing a video game.

Douglas Mitchell, a 58-year-old top-ranked archer from Scotland was killed with his own bow in 2002. Mitchell was handling the bow in his workshop when part of the assembly broke apart and struck Mitchell in the head.

South Korean boxer Duk Koo Kim was killed in the ring in 1982 after going fourteen rounds with Ray 'Boom Boom' Mancini. To minimize the risk of this ever happening again, the World Boxing Association shortened the maximum number of rounds from fifteen to twelve.

Ray Chapman, a baseball player for the Cleveland Indians, became the first (and still the only) major league player ever to be killed by a beanball (a ball aimed at the batter's head). The unintentionally fatal pitch came from Yankees pitcher Carl Mays in 1920.

✦

Problematic baseball player Ed Delahanty was suspended in 1903 by the Washington Nationals for a number of violations. He decided to take a trip to get away from the conflict, and boarded a train to Niagara Falls. Ordered off the train for drunk and disorderly conduct, he fell through a drawbridge and into Niagara Falls.

✦

In 1964, Mark Maples became the first person to be killed in Disneyland. As the Matterhorn bobsled he was riding reached the top of the mountain, Mark undid his seat belt and stood up. He was promptly hurled onto the tracks below.

✦

While competing in the 1958 Tour of Gippsland in Melbourne, Australia cyclist and two-times Olympic medalist Russell Mockridge died just two miles from the start of the race. He had been hit by an oncoming bus.

✦

British racing driver J. G. Parry-Thomas was decapitated in 1927 when his car's drive chain snapped and whipped into the cockpit. Despite being headless and burned to cinders in the ensuing crash, Parry-Thomas was hailed in the next day's newspapers for having set a new speed record of 180 miles per hour.

❧

'Ghost riding the whip' is a relatively new automotive sport that is rapidly gaining popularity, particularly among West Coast fans of hip-hop music. 'Ghost riding' refers to traveling in a car with no driver; 'whip' is urban slang for automobile. Ghost riders typically put the car in neutral, get out, and begin dancing around or on top of the slow-moving vehicle. Sometimes they just let go of the wheel and stick their bodies out of the car.

Davender Gulley of Stockton, California was very good at ghost riding, until his head slammed into a parked car while he was hanging out of the window of his SUV.

❧

At the 1977 South African Grand Prix, track marshal Jansen Van Vuuren ran across the track with a fire extinguisher to attend to a race car that had caught fire. Before he got to the other side of the track, he was hit by the Formula One car being driven by Tom Pryce. Van Vuuren died on impact. Pryce, who had survived the fire, was killed when the fire extinguisher flew out of Van Vuuren's hands and hit Pryce in the face.

❧

An online virtual reality game enthusiast named Qiu Chengwei was sentenced to death in Shanghai in 2005 for fatally stabbing his friend. The two had argued over the rightful ownership of an imaginary sword.

At a horse race in Loreto, Mexico in 2006, the two front-runners were approaching the finish line neck-and-neck. A young man named José Bernardo González suddenly jumped from the stands and stood in the path of the oncoming horses. From what friends and witnesses could later gather, it appeared that González wanted to make sure that the horse he had bet on would win. The only sure thing that day was González's skull getting crushed in the stampede.

In 1996, David Bailey of Clondalkin, Ireland went to retrieve a golf ball from a ditch near the first hole. His sudden approach frightened a rat, which ran up his trouser leg and peed on him. His friends urged Bailey to go back to the clubhouse and shower, but he assured them it was no big deal. He wiped the urine off and seeing no bites or scratches, continued with the game. A week later, Bailey was dead of kidney failure brought on by a case of the rare but deadly Weil's disease.

Tom and Eileen Lonergan of Louisiana were on a scuba-diving expedition in 1998 in the shark-infested waters off Australia's Great Barrier Reef. The boat that had taken their group of divers out to sea inadvertently left the Lonergans behind. The two were never seen again.

❧

The World Wrestling Federation had arranged for Owen Hart to win a match in 1999. In typically splashy style, Hart was lowered into the ring from the stadium rafters, clad brilliantly in his Blue Blazer costume, replete with cape and feathers. With less than 80 feet to go, the cable snapped loose. Owen entered the ring with a splat in front of 16,000 fans. The ecstatic crowd roared, thinking it was part of the show. After several minutes, the master of ceremonies announced, 'Folks, we've got a problem here.'

❧

Otto Lilienthal was a German pioneer in the earliest days of aviation. Wilbur and Orville Wright used many of Lilienthal's calculations on lift and aerodynamics in the early 1900s, despite some errors that sent the Wright brothers back to the drawing board on numerous occasions. In 1896, while experimenting with a hang glider he had just designed, Lilienthal crashed into a field. He died of his injuries two days later.

❧

Georgi Markov was a Bulgarian dissident and Olympic weight-lifting gold medalist. In 1978, an unidentified man with an accent stepped out of a London crowd and shot Markov in the leg with a specially rigged umbrella. The pellet that embedded itself in Markov's calf was full of ricin poison. The assassin got away in a taxi.

Thinning the Herd

※

An empty inflatable kayak washed up early one morning in 2007 on a beach in Kaikoura, New Zealand. There was some fishing gear on board, an empty potato chip bag, and a half-drunk soda bottle on the floor, but no other sign of the kayak's owner. An astute police sergeant told the press, 'Indications are that a person should have been with it.'

※

One of the strangest spectator sports in all of history has to be jumper-gawking at the Mihara-Yama volcano in Japan. It began as a twisted sort of spiritual journey in 1933, when 24-year-old Mieko Ueki painted a lovely image in words for her friend, Masako Tomita. Standing at the lip of the volcano, Mieko told Masako that jumping into the bubbling lava would be a beautiful way to die - instantly cremated and then rising to heaven in a billowing swirl of smoke. Masako protested a bit, but then agreed not to interfere. The two young women bowed respectfully to one another. Masako stepped aside, and Mieko jumped in.

News of the 'poetic suicide' spread quickly, and inspired nearly a thousand others to leap into the stinking lava. Many thousands more came to watch. Steamship service to the volcano doubled. Roadside stands, tourist stops, hotels, and restaurants popped up all over the place. The Japanese government eventually limited access to the area, but not until the economy had been given a fair chance to benefit from this unexpected boom.

It took thirty-five years for divers to recover the remains of Donald Campbell and his Bluebird boat from the bottom of Coniston Water in Cumbria. Campbell had been trying to break his own speed record in 1967. As he approached his previous top speed of 276 miles per hour, the boat gracefully rose out of the water, did a few quadruple backflips, and then sank nose-first, 150 feet below the surface of the lake. Campbell remained in radio contact while his boat completed its gymnastics routine. 'I can't see much, the water's very bad indeed . . . I'm getting a lot of bloody row in here . . . I've got the bows up . . . I've gone.'

9

BETTER LUCK NEXT TIME

EVERYBODY KNOWS THAT THE GREAT RUSSIAN POET MAIAKOVSKY
COMMITTED SUICIDE. WHAT IS NOT SO WELL KNOWN IS THAT
HIS LAST WORDS WERE, 'COMRADES, DON'T SHOOT.'
Fred Botten

THERE HAVE BEEN *times, while doing the dishes, for example, that
a glass has slipped through my soapy fingers, dropped into the sink,
ricocheted off a dish, bounced onto the counter, then plunged to the floor,
only to survive the harrowing experience with nary a scratch. Another glass
from the same set may shatter into a million pieces if I so much
as drop an ice cube into it the wrong way. People can be equally fragile,
and just as mind-bogglingly resilient. Against all odds, and no matter
how right it would otherwise be, some of them just won't die.*

In 2005, a 21-year-old man from Murdoch, Australia created a beer-drinking device that consisted of a helmet connected to a keg via a hose, and powered by an electric drill. The contraption, he hoped, would allow him to consume large quantities of beer in record time. The force with which the beer shot out of the keg ripped open the man's stomach. Amazingly, he lived.

❧

In 2004, a man registered as a guest at The Inn at Bingham School in Mebane, North Carolina was hoping to die quietly in a beautiful, peaceful place. Once in his room, he disconnected the propane gas line attached to the fireplace and lay himself down on the soft, comfortable bed. He blew up the historic home, and suffered only minor burns in the explosion.

❧

Porn star Mary Carey was forced to drop out of the 2003 California governor's race against Arnold Schwarzenegger when her mother jumped off the roof of a four-story building in Florida. The mother survived. Mary's political career did not.

❧

Distraught over the belief that his wife was having an affair, Alfonse Mumbo of Kenya cut off his own penis and testicles with a kitchen knife in 2003. Unfortunately for him, he lived. Mrs. Mumbo denied ever having an affair.

❧

In 2007, an Atlanta apartment manager was handed a letter by two of her tenants. She soon realized that the letter was a suicide note and immediately contacted the police. The tenants, two men in their early forties, were distraught over the failure of their business. The officers arrived to find the apartment soaked in blood, a circular saw buzzing, and three of the men's four arms on the floor. Police turned off the saw before the second man could cut off his other arm. Both men survived.

❧

A 47-year-old Munich man tried to end it all by jumping in front of a train. He missed. He smashed instead through the window of the engine car, seriously frightening the train conductor. The trauma caused the conductor to miss several weeks of work. The courts ordered the man to pay for repairs to the train, and for the conductor's lost wages.

A Florida man shot a ring-necked duck in 2007 and stored it in a freezer for later consumption. Two days later, the man's wife opened the freezer and was scared nearly to death when the duck placidly lifted its head and looked at her. The duck, now known as Perky, was transported to Goose Creek Wildlife Sanctuary, where she was treated for wounds to her wing and leg. During surgery, however, Perky suffered cardiac arrest. She was successfully resuscitated, thereby cheating death yet again.

A man from New South Wales, Australia convinced himself that he was dying of a communicable disease and that he had already infected his wife and children. To spare himself and his family this terrible fate, he decided they should all die. In the middle of his homemade crime spree, he called the police to notify them of the murder-suicide in progress. While waiting for the cops to arrive, he stabbed himself repeatedly, but found that he wasn't dying quickly enough. So he hit himself over the head with a hammer a few times. Police arrived to find the man hiding in a garden shed, severely battered, but still alive.

When a magazine prematurely published Rudyard Kipling's obituary in the 1930s, he wrote them a short note: 'I've just read that I am dead. Don't forget to delete me from your list of subscribers.'

❧

A 37-year-old Dutch man suffering from hypothermia was hospitalized in The Hague in 2001 after he jumped from a bridge - three times. Police found him leaning over the railing of the bridge, shivering and frostbitten, and about to plunge into the icy waters for the fourth time. Despite the man's obvious determination, it is unclear why he didn't try a different method after the first attempt failed.

❧

In 2006, Amy Dallamura from Aberystwyth was issued with an ASBO banning her from her favourite beach resort, its promenade and the surrounding area after being rescued several times from drowning. One emergency rescue technician almost lost his own life trying to save her when he had to let go of his safety line to swim out an additional 300 meters. Ms. Dallamura was terribly upset over the banishment. She said she never asked to be rescued. She was merely seeking to end her back pain.

❧

The British magazine *Melody Maker* took an unusual approach in reviewing an Alice Cooper concert in the 1970s. The critic wrote the review in the form of an obituary. The undisputed king of 'shock rock,' whose gory onstage shenanigans and signature horror-film makeup won him millions of fans worldwide, later issued the following statement: 'I'm alive, and drunk as usual.'

≋

During a 2003 Ku Klux Klan initiation ritual in Tennessee, Gregory Freeman fired several shots into the air. Perhaps not fully grasping the concept of gravity, he never considered that what goes up must come down. The descending bullet struck fellow Klansman Jeff Murr on the head, wounding him critically.

≋

A Romanian doctor was treated for severe shock when he was attacked in the morgue by what he thought was a corpse. Bogdan Georgescu, aged sixteen, had collapsed while drinking coffee with his brother and was taken to Brasov County Hospital, where he was declared dead on arrival. Some time later, the teenager opened his eyes and found himself surrounded by dead people. When he saw a man in a white coat approaching, he panicked and began swinging. The doctor was given a few days off to recover from the scare and the beating.

≋

James McNeill Whistler, creator of the famous 1871 painting known commonly as *Whistler's Mother*, was reported dead in a Dutch newspaper after he suffered a heart attack. Whistler graciously thanked the Dutch newspaper in a note saying, 'Reading my own obituary induced a tender glow of health.'

✈

Convicted murderer Ruben Dario Ovejero of Tucuman, Argentina was released from prison in 2005 when the man he was accused of killing strolled back into town one fine April day, drunk but still alive. Pedro Roldan told police that he had no idea people thought he was dead.

✈

A woman from Nuremberg, Germany called the police one night, alarmed when her boyfriend became suddenly silent while she was talking to him on the phone. Emergency services dispatched a police car, firefighters, and an ambulance to the man's house. The blaring sirens brought the man to the door, where he told officers that he had dozed off during a lull in the conversation.

✈

About twenty people each year visit the beautiful white chalk cliffs of Beachy Head in East Sussex and jump to their deaths. A few others are thrown. In July of 2002, one young man took a leap and landed on a ledge about halfway down. He called the coastguard on his cell phone and asked them to pick him up; he had changed his mind.

Abe Vigoda, the elderly, tall, slouching actor known to fans of the 1970s show *Barney Miller* and who played 'Sal Tessio' in the film *The Godfather,* is periodically reported dead by a number of US publications. His current state (dead or alive) is continuously updated on his Internet website, www.abevigoda.com.

❧

Dave Swarbrick, a British folk-music fiddler, read his own obituary in a 1999 edition of *The Daily Telegraph*. Swarbrick took the news with characteristic good humor. 'It's not the first time I have died in Coventry,' he said.

❧

Gary Davies's dog burst into flames when it peed on a live wire. Davies later told the press, 'There was an almighty explosion, and the whole street lit up. I turned round, and the dog was on fire.' Power was off for five hours that day in Middlestone Moor in Durham. Against all odds, the dog survived.

❧

Louise Egan Brunstad, a lovesick and suicidal sixteen-year-old girl from Atlanta, Georgia, crashed her car into an oncoming vehicle in 2006. She counted down the seconds before impact in text messages she sent to the female classmate who spurned her. The girl survived. The unfortunate driver of the other car did not.

Thinning the Herd

❧

The family of Julia Warnes received a letter from her utilities company in 2006, advising them to make arrangements to have billing and water services discontinued now that she was dead. Julia had suffered complications during surgery some weeks prior. She herself called the company and told them that she would still need water, especially considering that she was still alive.

❧

Christina Mack of Peoria, Illinois greased the floor of her kitchen in an attempt to kill her one-legged boyfriend in 1997. She slipped on the floor and knocked herself unconscious instead. Police found more grease near the top of the stairs and by the bathroom door. The boyfriend, Chester Parkman Sr., insisted that Christina was just doing a little housework.

❧

Master prankster Alan Abel loved staging elaborate hoaxes. Despite having been exposed as a fraud several times over a period of forty years, he was remarkably successful in making otherwise successful and respected people look like dopes. In 1979, he faked his own death to get *The New York Times* to write his obituary. They did. The following day, Abel held a press conference in which he borrowed a line from Mark Twain: 'Reports of my demise have been grossly exaggerated.'

Benjamin Franklin had a long-standing yet friendly feud with Titan Leeds, who published an almanac that competed with Franklin's *Poor Richard's Almanac*. Franklin made predictions of the date of Leeds's demise in 1733, 1734, 1735, and 1740. Each time the date came and went with Leeds still alive, Franklin published his obituary in his newspaper anyway. Leeds responded every time by writing Franklin letters 'from the great beyond.'

10

WHEN THE FUR FLIES

KINKY IS USING A FEATHER. PERVERTED IS
USING THE WHOLE CHICKEN.
Author unknown

EVERY YEAR, *at the start of deer-hunting season, the editor of a local newspaper in Upstate New York, sets up a tally board in his office: Deer versus People. I'm not sure if the season has ever ended with more dead people than deer, but I find the idea of someone keeping such a score-card rather amusing, and oddly comforting. I'm rooting for the deer, of course, and I suspect that editor is as well.*

Dozens of angry fishermen gathered regularly to try to exact their revenge on Kuno, a 77-pound catfish that leapt out of the water and killed a dachshund in 2001. The pet wiener dog had made the terrible mistake one day of going for a swim in Kuno's lake. Kuno ate him.

For more than two years, Kuno managed to evade capture. However, he was no match for Mother Nature. A drought turned Kuno's pond into not much more than a muddy bog. The fishermen were at last able to trudge right up to the 5-foot-long dog-eater and pluck him out of the shallow waters. Kuno was stuffed and mounted, and now resides above the mantle in a nearby lodge in Mönchengladbach, Germany.

A sparrow flew through an open window at a Dutch convention centre in 2005 and knocked over 23,000 dominoes. An angry mob cornered the poor, frightened bird, and someone shot it. The senseless killing sparked the outrage of millions around the world. In response, Dutch authorities announced that the sparrow would be preserved as a national treasure. The bird can now be seen at Rotterdam's Natural History Museum, perched on top of a box of dominoes.

Thinning the Herd

In a show of incomprehensible extravagance, the Roman poet Virgil arranged a funeral for his pet housefly. Virgil spent the modern equivalent of £50,000 on the ceremony, a catered affair that was held in his mansion, replete with orchestra and paid mourners.

It is said that Pond Square in London is haunted by the ghost of the chicken that was killed by Sir Francis Bacon in the seventeenth century. The English philosopher, statesman, and essayist had been riding in an open-air carriage through the snowy streets of London with his friend Dr. Witherborne, debating whether cold could be used to preserve meat as effectively as salt. In a spur-of-the moment decision to conduct the experiment right then and there, Sir Francis jumped out of the carriage and bought a hen from a local woman. The bird was killed, and Sir Francis immediately proceeded to stuff it with snow. Bacon died of pneumonia before confirming whether the experiment was a success, but many people in the centuries since have reported hearing a strange screeching in the middle of the night and the ghostly apparitions of a frantic chicken in Pond Square.

In 1834, Scottish botanist David Douglas fell into a concealed pit trap in Hawaii. He might have survived the fall, but was crushed to death by the wild bull that fell into the pit right after him.

※

In its efforts to eradicate malaria in Malaysia in the 1950s, the World Health Organisation orchestrated what was perhaps the largest-ever massacre of animals and insects resulting from a single act. After careful study and consideration, they ordered the spraying of DDT over a vast region of the country. This killed off a significant portion of the malaria-carrying mosquitoes, but created a few other problems. First, people's houses began to fall down on top of their heads; it turned out that, along with the mosquitoes, the DDT had also killed the wasps, which allowed their favourite food source - thatch-eating caterpillars - to thrive. Hundreds of thousands of geckos then arrived to devour the billions of dead mosquitoes and wasps. Residual DDT from the insects didn't kill the geckos, but it did give them a severe neurological disorder. In came the cats to feast on the slow-moving geckos. Unfortunately, the consumption of DDT-infected lizards began killing the cats. As the cats disappeared, the rat population exploded. Although malaria was no longer a huge problem for the humans in the region, thanks to the rats, there was now plenty of typhus and plague to go around.

In order to restore ecological balance to the area, the World Health Organisation determined that the best course of action would be to air-drop 14,000 live cats into Borneo via parachute. Before long, the mosquito population prospered once again.

※

Greek philosopher Chrysippus is believed to have died of laughter in 207 BC after watching his drunken donkey attempt to eat figs.

Thinning the Herd

Maurice John McCredden of Manjimup, Australia, was killed in 2006 when an airborne kangaroo crashed through the windshield of his car. It was not clear whether the kangaroo died in the crash, or if it was already dead when it hit McCredden's car.

⁊ಠ

A customs officer stopped Wayne Floyd as he was about to board a flight from Sydney, Australia to Bangkok, Thailand. There was something suspicious about the weird bulge in Floyd's crotch. A strip search revealed that he was attempting to smuggle six eggs from an endangered species in his underwear. Two of the creatures died in Floyd's makeshift nest. Floyd was sentenced in 2006.

⁊ಠ

There are many theories surrounding the death of the author Edgar Allan Poe, including that he died either of alcoholism, epilepsy, a diabetic coma, brain fever, or as a result of a beating from a band of thugs. He was found in a state of delirium outside a Baltimore tavern wearing tattered clothing that didn't belong to him. He died the following morning, on 7 October 1849, in a Washington D.C. hospital. Based on a modern-day analysis of his state and the symptoms noted in his medical records, the most likely cause of Poe's death is that he was bitten by a wild animal and died of rabies.

＊

US Vice President Dick Cheney single-handedly killed more than seventy farm-raised ring-necked pheasants during a 2003 hunting expedition. Along with nine other companions, the men killed a total of 417 pheasants and an undisclosed number of mallard ducks. The birds had been cleverly placed in the controlled environment of a 'canned hunt' to make the experience a little less taxing for the vice president and his guests.

Perhaps not wanting to reignite the outrage of impassioned animal advocates, Cheney participated in another hunting expedition three years later, this time in the wide-open spaces of a sprawling Texas ranch. The vice president mistook one of his hunting buddies for a quail, and nearly killed 78-year-old lawyer Harry Whittington of Austin, Texas. Despite the embedded bits of buckshot in his face and torso and the heart attack that followed, Whittington survived.

＊

Topsy was a 3-ton elephant whose great size and strength helped build many of the attractions at Coney Island's Luna Park, New York, in the late 1800s. Over time, however, Topsy developed a bad temper, the direct result of years of abuse and mishandling. She killed three men in three years.

Thompson and Dundy, who owned Luna Park, decided to make an example - not to mention a quick profit - at Topsy's expense. Shortly after the death of the last sadistic handler in 1903, they announced that Topsy was a menace to mankind and would be publicly hanged.

The ASPCA stepped in immediately, condemning the action. They pointed out that New York State had recently determined that death by hanging constituted cruel and unusual punishment, and had replaced the gallows with its first electric chair. So Thompson and Dundy asked Thomas Edison to arrange the execution. Edison, who had been experimenting on farm animals in his attempts to devise a more efficient electric chair, jumped at the chance to zap an elephant.

Sadly, Topsy was killed for the entertainment and profit of pitiless men. The only mercy was the fact that she died quickly. As fate would have it, however, Topsy got her revenge from beyond the grave. What was left of Luna Park was utterly destroyed in a massive fire of unknown origin in 1931. A memorial to Topsy now stands at the site where she died.

❧

For more than a hundred years, the labels on Tisbury Beer have contained the disclaimer, 'This bottle is guaranteed monkey proof.' The original head brewer had a pet monkey that drowned in a vat of beer.

❧

A shark caught in 1967 in the waters near Cheviot Beach in Australia was cut open and found empty. Rescuers were looking for Prime Minister Harold Holt, who disappeared when he went for a swim.

✎

A 23-foot-long python invaded a fruit orchard in Malaysia and ate eleven guard dogs over a period of several days in 2007. Villagers finally caught the enormous snake and tied it to a tree, where it remained until wildlife officials arrived to take it away.

✎

A possum ran across a power line near a New Zealand ski resort in 2007, electrocuting itself and bursting into flames. It took firefighters twelve hours to put out the kilometer-wide area of the mountainside that caught fire when the flaming animal fell to the ground.

✎

A Jack Russell terrier belonging to Andrew Turner, MP for the Isle of Wight, was held responsible for the murder of a polecat at a 2006 county fair. The terrier savagely shook the cat in its jaws, letting go only after someone threw a bucket of cold water on it.

✎

Villagers in Jakarta found two human hands, a leg, skull fragments, some hair, and a pair of shorts inside a 16-foot, half-ton crocodile in 2006. In accordance with local religious beliefs, they hacked the crocodile to pieces and ate it. This ritual is believed to prevent other crocodiles from eating any more villagers.

Thinning the Herd

❧

A group of Turkish aviation technicians sacrificed a camel on the tarmac of Istanbul's Atatürk International Airport in December 2006, in celebration of having finally gotten rid of the last of a series of problematic planes. The aircraft had been leased to Turkish Airlines by Britain, and their frequent breakdowns caused all manner of consternation to the technicians over a period of thirteen years. Turks traditionally sacrifice animals as thanks to God when their wishes come true.

❧

Franklyn Pigott Jr. from Cape Coral, Florida had tried everything to keep the bees off his property. In a last-ditch attempt, he mixed a product called Real Kill Indoor Fogger with the lubricant WD-40, and sprayed it on a nest of bees. The spray can turned into a flamethrower and destroyed the bees. It also set fire to Pigott's house.

❧

Fisherman Ian Card was ecstatic when he hooked an 800-pound, 14-foot blue marlin off the coast of Bermuda during a 2006 fishing tournament. The swordfish leapt into the boat, stabbed Card in the chest with its 3-foot razor-like snout, and pulled Card into the water with the hook still in its mouth. Card survived the attack. The fate of the marlin is unknown.

After eighteen years, Salim Khan finally received $13,500 from the Jaipur District of India as compensation for the 1988 vehicular homicide of his elephant. Babli, the 35-year-old pachyderm, had been Khan's only source of income. The Rajasthan High Court of Jaipur ruled that Babli was 'a living being,' as opposed to 'a livestock.' Khan told the press that he would use the money to buy a new elephant and go back to the business of giving elephant rides to tourists.

In 2002, a 61-year-old man ended his own life by climbing over a three-foot wall in a Portugal zoo and taunting the lions. Most of the lions in the pit ignored him for a while, but when a ten-year-old lioness had had enough of the man's shenanigans, she walked over to him and broke his neck.

Birds in Redding, California are particularly fond of the berry bushes that line Interstate 5. In the early spring of 2001, the berries began fermenting on the branches. Hundreds of inebriated birds began swooping down and flying erratically, crashing into windshields and dive-bombing into the pavement. No humans were reported hurt, but that area of the highway was littered with the avian victims of the alcoholic binge.

✤

Mocha the Labrador retriever was not the first dog to succumb to the irresistible lure of a hot spring at Yellowstone Park. In 2001, she bolted toward the bubbling pool the moment her family opened the doors of their motor home. Mocha realized her mistake as soon as she hit the 200°F water. Despite the brave rescue attempts of her heartbroken owner, Donald Hansen, Mocha didn't make it.

Accidental dog boiling occurs with alarming regularity at Yellowstone Park.

✤

One of the oldest known living creatures, Harriet the Tortoise, passed away at the ripe old age of 176 in an Australian zoo. Harriet was reputed to have been found on the Galapagos Islands in 1835 by none other than the father of evolutionary science, Charles Darwin. When he found her, she was estimated to be about five years old and was no bigger than a Frisbee. Darwin originally named her Harry, not realizing for several years that Harry was a girl.

✤

Sierra Stiles, an eight-year-old third-grader from Maryland landed the first kill of the 2005 bear hunting season. The little girl shot a 211-pound bear twice in the chest with her rifle. 'They won't eat now,' Sierra said of the bears. 'They won't eat a thing.'

In May 2006, Gabor Komlosy was dragged into the Szamos River in Hungary by a 150-pound catfish. The 53-year-old man's body was later found still clutching his fishing rod, despite the fact that he had bashed his head into a rock and had either drowned as a result, or his lungs had taken in water after he was dead. The catfish was no less obstinate than its would-be assassin; its mouth was still clamped firmly to the other end of the fishing line.

For all his careful and respected study of giant bears over a period of twenty-five years, Russian scientist Vitaly Nikolayenko learned the hard way that pepper spray doesn't work very well as a repellent on North American grizzlies. His bloodied and mangled body was discovered in 2003, inside a one-room hut in a desolate region near the Tikhaya River. Next to him were a giant paw print and an empty can of mace.

That same year, a self-proclaimed conservationist and documentary film-maker named Timothy Treadwell met a similar fate. While compiling film footage on the wild bears in Alaska, and despite his claims that he had been accepted by 'the clan' over the thirteen years he had been visiting the bears, parts of Treadwell and his girlfriend were discovered strewn throughout their camp. They were very small parts.

Thinning the Herd

11

JUST PLAIN WEIRD

WHEN I DIE, I'D LIKE TO BE SCATTERED OVER MY HOMETOWN.
BUT NOT, LIKE, CREMATED OR ANYTHING.
Mitch Berg

SOME PEOPLE LIVE *extraordinary lives - colorful, brilliant,
awe-inspiring, fabulously exotic, adventure-filled lives.
And then they die perfectly boring deaths.
None of them are in this chapter.*

Kyujiro Kanaoka of Japan was registered as Itami City's oldest living resident. Too bad he had been dead for ten years. His sons, all of whom were in their seventies, believed their father was just resting. They had left him more or less undisturbed on his futon for more than a decade. When authorities discovered the decomposed body of the elder Kanaoka in 2005, one of the sons told them that he had recently consulted a relative, suspecting something might be wrong with their father.

Pete Price, the host of the Merseyside talk show *Magic 1548*, became concerned when a frequent and terribly verbose caller, 'Terry' suddenly fell silent during a January 2006 broadcast. Price asked any listeners who might know Terry to find out what happened and render aid. Neighbors found Terry dead of a heart attack in his chair, with the phone still in his hand.

A Portuguese man wrote his last will and testament when he was twenty-nine years old. In it, he designated seventy beneficiaries, all of whom had been selected at random from the Lisbon telephone book. He passed away in 2007 at the age of forty-two, leaving the heirs he had never met approximately $11,000 each.

~~~

French prosecutors in the city of Rouen revealed that cannibalism was the most likely reason that some of the organs were missing from a dead prisoner. The suspected killer was a cellmate of the formerly intact convict. Under questioning, the suspect claimed to have eaten the victim's heart. What he ate, in fact, was part of the man's lung.

~~~

Former drug addict, thief, and regular all-around hoodlum Ravindra Kantrulu converted to Islam in 2006 and began murdering homosexuals. His wife, Anjali, boarded a train and traveled many miles with their youngest child in tow. She went to the police station in Raipur, India, to attest to her husband's innocence. Anjali claimed that the bloodied shirt and axe the police found in Ravindra's possession when they arrested him must have been planted there by corrupt officials. Also, she explained, her husband couldn't stand the sight of blood. Although Ravindra had already confessed to killing at least fifteen of the twenty-one victims, Anjali argued, 'He was very normal with me.'

~~~

The men who buried Attila the Hun and his treasures in AD 453 were put to death immediately upon their return so that the feared barbarian's grave would never be discovered.

❧

American volcanologist David A. Johnston was reporting on the 1980 eruption of Mount St. Helens in Washington State. Even if he had been standing several miles away, it still would have been too close. His last words were heard over a two-way radio: 'Vancouver, Vancouver, this is it!'

❧

Issei Sagawa, who was a student in Paris in 1981, invited a beautiful Dutch classmate, Renée Hartevelt, to his home for dinner. Shortly after she arrived, Sagawa killed her. Then he ate her.

❧

William Kogut was a Californian death-row inmate in the 1930s. Believing he could fashion an execution for himself that was less horrific than any the State had in store for him, Kogut unscrewed a hollow steel leg from his cot and packed it tightly with torn pieces of playing cards, which Kogut knew were printed with ink that contained a very volatile material. He poured water into the other end of the tube and placed the device between his head and the gas heater in his cell. As the heated water turned into steam, pressure built up in the tube. The ensuing explosion was powerful enough to blow a hole through Kogut's skull, in effect making him the first prisoner to execute himself using a pipe bomb, and perhaps the only person ever to blow his brains out with a deck of playing cards.

In January 1919, a 30-foot 'wall of goo' swept through Boston, killing 21 people and injuring 150 others. Unseasonably warm temperatures caused a giant tank filled with molasses to burst open and spew two million gallons of the sticky substance all over the center of the city. The massive wave destroyed buildings, swallowed up horses, and swept away wagons and everything else in its path. Rescue efforts were nearly impossible; rescuers were either carried away in the thick wave or became hopelessly stuck in the syrup.

A pig farmer from Vancouver became Canada's deadliest serial killer in 2007. Willie Pickton murdered and dismembered forty-nine women in his slaughterhouse. He told an undercover police officer that he wanted to kill one more, to bring the total to a nice even fifty.

In September 2006, a group of masked men in military garb burst into the *Sol y Sombra* bar in Mexico and tossed five human heads into a crowd of dancers. Beheadings have become rather commonplace throughout Mexico in recent years, as a way of intimidating police and exacting vengeance on rival drug dealers and other enemies.

In 2006, 27-year-old Jason Chellow of rural Placer County, California, was killed by his own house. Although the house was built in the 1980s, no one knew that it had been constructed over a long-defunct mine. As Jason entered the kitchen, a giant hole opened up and sucked him underground. It took rescuers several days to extract the man's body from the cave-in.

The toasty-warm skeleton of a forty-year-old woman was found in her London bedsit in January 2006. Joyce Vincent was on the floor surrounded by half-wrapped Christmas presents, lying between a heater and the television set. Both appliances were still running. Police believed she had been dead for three years. She was discovered by housing trust officials who, after two years of unpaid rent, had decided to repossess.

A US World War II bomber plane named *Lady Be Good* crash-landed in the desert in Libya in 1943. Sixteen years later, oil surveyors from Britain stumbled on the wreckage that had been extraordinarily well preserved by the dry climate. The machine guns, radio, and one of the engines still worked, and there were several containers of fresh water on board. There was, however, no sign of the nine crew members who had been on this flight.

The Air Force did not take the sighting seriously when it was first reported by the oil surveyors. It would be another year

Thinning the Herd

before they sent a search team to the site. In 1960, the wreckage and the mummified remains of eight of the nine crew-members were finally located.

Parts of *Lady Be Good* are still on display at the Army Quartermaster Museum in Fort Lee, Virginia. Through the years, night watchmen have reported hearing voices and eerie sounds near the display, and that pieces of the plane often move by themselves.

❧

Actor Gareth Jones collapsed and died while in make-up between scenes in a live television play in 1958 in Manchester. Director Ted Kotcheff continued the play to its conclusion, improvising around Jones's absence.

❧

Actor Paul Mantz was a flying prodigy in the early twentieth century. He came out of retirement in 1965 to work as a stunt pilot in *Flight of the Phoenix*, the story of crash survivors who attempt to construct a new aircraft from pieces of the wreckage. Mantz successfully landed the pieced-together airplane during the first test run. While filming the second attempt, the plane failed to clear a sand dune. Mantz was decapitated when the engine broke away.

❧

William Bullock was killed in 1867 by his own invention, the web rotary press. A driving belt came off its pulley, so Bullock kicked the machine to get it going again. The press swallowed his leg and then proceeded to mangle it. The leg became gangrenous within a few days. Bullock died during the amputation procedure intended to save his life.

❧

Detective Allan Pinkerton, considered America's first great detective, tripped on a pavement in 1884 and bit off a bit of his tongue. He died of the ensuing infection.

❧

Leslie Harvey, guitarist of Stone the Crows, was electrocuted onstage during a concert in Wales in 1972. The plug on the microphone was not grounded. Unfortunately, Harvey was.

❧

A truck driver identified only as 'Martin T' suffocated to death under 16,000 pounds of manure. The 34-year-old man was in the process of dumping the load in a field near the western Czech city of Karlovy Vary.

❧

Massachusetts inmate Michelle Kosilek, who was Robert Kosilek when he went to prison, petitioned the federal courts to have the government pay for the final steps in his sex-change surgery. Kosilek said that being trapped in a man's body was like 'the dying I do inside a little bit every day.' Kosilek's wife, on the other hand did all her dying at once. He had strangled her to death with a piano wire in 1990.

❧

Chef Bernard Loiseau was very proud of his restaurant's hard-won three-star Michelin rating. In 2003, however, French restaurant guide *Gault Millau*, downgraded chef Loiseau's rating from 19 to 17 on their own review scale. Loiseau was beside himself, distraught over the possibility that this review might cause him to lose one of his Michelin stars, making his restaurant merely 'very, very good.' He put a shotgun to his head and blew his brains out.

❧

Russian cosmonaut Yuri Gagarin was the first man in space and one of his country's greatest heroes. During a training exercise on the new MiG-15UTI rocket in 1968, Gagarin crashed just outside of Moscow. They found his body hours later, frozen and reeking of alcohol.

✢

Pizza delivery man Brian Wells was as dependable as he was predictable. His daily routine was invariable, and he had never been in trouble with the law. In 2003, while standing outside the bank he had just robbed, he told police officers surrounding him that he had been kidnapped by three people and coerced into committing this crime. A simple pipe bomb was elaborately locked around his neck. Wells begged police to let him go because the kidnappers had set the bomb to go off minutes after the well-planned robbery. While they waited for the bomb squad to arrive, the device exploded, instantly killing Wells.

✢

A Greek family quickly canceled their holiday plans shortly after arriving at their hotel room. The father walked over to one of the beds to inspect a strange lump under the covers, which turned out to be a severed human head.

✢

In case you missed it, the secret behind Victoria's Secret, women's underwear brand was that 'Victoria' was a man named Roy Raymond. The other interesting thing about Roy Raymond was that he jumped to his death from the Golden Gate Bridge in 1993.

Thinning the Herd

❧

The families of British tourists Andrew Redfern and Louis Selo - who had never met and whose sons died under completely different circumstances in two different countries - faced a strangely similar problem. Andrew died in October 2006 after falling on his forehead in a hotel lobby in Cuba. Louis died of a heart attack one month earlier, while on holiday in Dublin. Andrew was returned to England without his lungs, kidneys, and part of his brain. Louis was sent back with two hearts and four lungs. The families are still waiting for a believable explanation.

❧

Absurdist French playwright Alfred Jarry was the inventor of *pataphysique*, the science of imaginary solutions. He often wandered the streets of Paris under a bright green umbrella, wearing cycling gear and two guns, and speaking in the high falsetto voice of one of his characters. He died at the age of thirty-four in 1907, the net result of alcoholism and tuberculosis. His last words were, 'I am dying. Please, bring me a toothpick.'

❧

An elderly man from Adelaide, Australia returned home from a short vacation and found a naked dead man in his bathroom. The twenty-year-old intruder had broken into the man's home and helped himself to some prescription pills. The drugs turned out to be diabetes medication.

Certain Christian sects incorporate snake handling into their religious services. Believers in this practice state that no harm will come to a snake handler who is 'right with God.'

In the spring of 2006, the Reverend Dwayne Long of Jonesville, Virginia, incorporated a snake-handling segment into his church's Easter Sunday service. He was killed by the venomous rattlesnake. When church members later were asked whether they thought Reverend Long was not 'right with God,' they explained, 'It was just his time to go.'

12

DEATHS FORETOLD

THE FUTURE WILL BE BETTER TOMORROW.
J. Danforth Quayle,
former Vice President of the United States

I AM OCCASIONALLY *plagued by the suspicion that some of the people who have been locked up in psychiatric facilities or who hear voices that others do not, may in fact be more evolved than we know, attuned to some wavelength the rest of us have never learned to access. Maybe we lock them up because we're jealous of the fact that no one occupies the empty rooms in our own heads. Or maybe they really are nuts.*

Several of the *Titanic's* staff and crew either failed to show up, resigned their posts, or ignored premonitions of disaster – their own or those of their loved ones. Some were just the happy beneficiaries of dumb luck.

- Second Engineer Colin MacDonald turned down the offer to join the crew of the *Titanic* because of a 'gut feeling' that something was going to go wrong.

- Crewman Bertrand Slade missed his train and arrived after *Titanic* had set sail.

- Luigi Gatta, manager of the controller's office for *Titanic*, dismissed his wife's comments about 'feeling strange' about the ship's maiden voyage.

- John Morgan, owner of the ship, became suddenly ill and was unable to sail.

Others who missed the launch or canceled at the last minute include the following:

- Millionaire George Vanderbilt canceled his plans the night before the trip, claiming a longtime superstitious fear of being on a ship's maiden voyage. It was, in fact, his mother-in-law who had sent an urgent telegram begging him to change his plans. Vanderbilt's luggage was on board when the ship sank.

- Robert Bacon, US ambassador to Paris, claimed 'last-minute business' and canceled his trip.

- Frank Adelman and his wife sailed on a later ship after Mrs. Adelman convinced her husband that they must not travel on *Titanic*.

- Henry Frick canceled his trip after his wife sprained her ankle. It wasn't a serious injury, but it served as a convenient and believable excuse for changing their minds so soon before sailing.

- James O'Brien canceled because he had witnessed a robbery and was ordered to testify in court in Ireland.

- Edward Bill's wife was yet another one of many spouses who begged their husbands not to travel on this ship. He heeded the warning and survived.

❧

In 1914, John Howlet, a Newfoundland sealer, told his wife of a chilling nightmare in which he was on a mountain of ice, terrified, lost, and freezing, surrounded by vague, indefinable 'things.' Two weeks later, Howlet was among 120 sealers abandoned on an ice floe in the North Atlantic after a horrific shipwreck. The missing men were not discovered for two days, by which time more than half the men were dead. Howlet was one of the lucky few who survived.

❧

In 1898, fourteen years before the *Titanic* disaster, author Morgan Robertson published the novel *Futility*. The novel was about a ship named *Titan*. It was nearly the same size as *Titanic* and carried almost the same number of passengers. Each ship, the real one and the fictitious one, struck an iceberg in the North Atlantic in mid-April and sank, with the loss of over half of their passengers due to insufficient lifeboats.

Another author, W. T. Stead, also wrote numerous stories and articles predicting that a large ocean liner would sink with the loss of over half on board due to the lack of sufficient lifeboats. Stead, an avid believer that the ghosts of the dead roamed among the living, received three separate warnings that travel would be dangerous in the month of April 1912. One such warning came from a very live person, a clergyman who wrote to Stead predicting a catastrophe on water. Despite these warnings, Stead booked passage on the *Titanic* and died in the disaster.

❧

For months before his death, country music singer Johnny Horton was haunted by ominous premonitions that he would be killed by a drunk. While waiting to perform at the Skyline Club in Texas

Thinning the Herd

in November 1960, he became nearly hysterical when bandmates suggested they hang out at the bar. He hid far away from the bar, certain his killer was waiting for him there. After the show, the band loaded their gear into Horton's Cadillac, and he headed home to Shreveport, Louisiana, wanting nothing more than to put Texas behind him. On the way, a truck crashed into Horton's Cadillac on a bridge in Milano, Texas, killing the singer. The driver of the truck was charged with intoxication manslaughter.

The eerie coincidences of Horton's life did not end there. The Skyline Club was where his friend, Hank Williams, had performed his last show. Williams also died in a car accident after that performance. Horton became close with his widow, Billie Jean, and married her the following year. Billie Jean became a musician's widow twice, having lost both husbands in the same way after having performed at the same club.

❧

A woman scheduled to board a transatlantic passenger ship became inexplicably queasy and anxious the moment she laid eyes on the luxury liner. The day before launch, the ship's mascot, a small black cat, ran away and was never seen again; several crewmen were heard to remark that this was a particularly bad omen. Another passenger who had booked passage on the ship, a successful shoe dealer from Boston, canceled his passage the day before the trip, finding himself unaccountably concerned and frightened. The ship was the *Lusitania*, sunk during World War I by a German torpedo in May of 1915. Nearly 1,200 people lost their lives in that tragedy.

꙳

David Booth had a vivid and recurring dream ten nights in a row. He dreamt of an American Airlines flight taking off on a sunny day, its nose pointing straight up but making a noise that didn't seem right. The plane suddenly banked to one side, dived toward the ground, and exploded in an enormous ball of fire. Each time, David awoke from this dream full of overwhelming despair.

Plagued by the notion that he should do something about this and knowing he might be dismissed as just another kook, David nonetheless contacted the FAA and recounted his dream to an official over the phone. Without details regarding a specific place and time, there was nothing anyone could do.

On the morning of 25 May 1979, David awoke with the certainty that he would never have this dream again. It was on that very day that American Airlines flight 191 crashed in a field near the runway at O'Hare Airport shortly after takeoff. The incident happened in a manner the thirty-year FAA official who had spoken to David Booth would later describe as 'eerily accurate.'

꙳

The tristate area near the shared borders of Missouri, Oklahoma, and Kansas is known as the Spooksville Triangle. Almost every night for the past hundred and fifty years, a strange ball of light can be seen bouncing along a road known as Devil's Promenade. As it moves, it leaves behind a trail of luminous sparks. Many scientists have studied this phenomenon but have never been able to agree on an explanation. Residents of the area refer to the light as The Devil's Jack-o'-Lantern

A flight attendant scheduled to fly on Eastern Airlines flight 401 had a strong premonition of danger and refused to go as scheduled. She also managed to convince her crew not to take that flight. That plane crashed into the Florida Everglades in 1972, killing 101 of the 172 passengers and crew on board.

Bernadette Soubirous was a poor French girl who saw a vision of the Virgin Mary at a grotto in Lourdes. Her body was exhumed several times in the decades following her death and was found to be incorruptible - a term that describes a corpse that shows no signs of decomposition long after it should have turned to dust. The Catholic Church considers the incorruptibility of a corpse to be one of the signs of sainthood.

At the site of Bernadette's vision, The Lady instructed the young girl to dig into the dry, barren earth with her bare hands. A spring of fresh water miraculously emerged. Countless millions have visited the grotto since 1862, with many reporting recoveries from devastating illnesses and injuries after drinking or touching water from the spring.

Despite having contracted a painfully debilitating bone disease some years later, Bernadette was informed by The Lady that the water would never heal her, so she never sought relief for her own suffering at the grotto.

Bernadette died at the age of thirty-five at the Convent of Nevers. Her body was exhumed in 1909, thirty years after her death, and found to be incorruptible. Her clothing was damp and she was sprinkled with sawdust from the rotting casket, but the corpse itself was intact, and actually emitted a sweet fragrance.

Bernadette was exhumed and re-examined in 1919, and then again in 1925. Except for a darkening of her skin that might have occurred during the first exhumation when nuns bathed her and changed her clothes, there was hardly a change in the condition of her corpse. She was finally placed in a crystal coffin in a chapel at the Convent of Nevers. Her body has been on view ever since, and can still be seen bearing the remarkable appearance of fresh youth.

13

HMM

ALWAYS GO TO OTHER PEOPLE'S FUNERALS.
OTHERWISE, THEY WON'T COME TO YOURS.
Yogi Berra

ONCE YOU'VE SEEN *Britney Spears emerge from a limo without
a scrap of underwear to cover what's left of her dignity, you realize
one important thing: death is the only real taboo left.*

The custom of covering the face of a dead person with a sheet evolved from an ancient pagan ritual. People believed that a person's spirit escapes through the mouth at the time of death. In an effort to keep the spirit inside the body and possibly delay death, they would hold the dying person's mouth and nose shut. This surely finished off more pagans than whatever disease was killing them.

***

As of the end of 2006, nearly two hundred people had been 'buried' in outer space. Through an agreement with NASA, commercial service organizations can arrange for a small sample of a deceased person's cremains to be launched into space during an already-scheduled space shuttle mission. The ashes are placed in a container about the size of a lipstick tube, and then released while the rocket is orbiting the Earth, the moon, or even as far away as Pluto. In the cheap version of the service, the tubes eventually return to Earth through the planet's gravitational pull, then burn up and disintegrate during reentry.

Some famous persons buried in space include Gene Roddenberry (*Star Trek* creator), Timothy Leary (hippie and philosopher), James Doohan ('Scotty' from *Star Trek*), and Leroy Gordon Cooper Jr. (one of the original Mercury Seven astronauts).

The Japanese are perhaps the only culture that regards suicide as an honorable way to resolve particularly embarrassing predicaments. About 30,000 people kill themselves each year in Japan. Despite the deeply ingrained mores of tradition and the apparent lack of horror over such an act (compared to other nations and cultures), there have been calls to ban certain best-selling books that glorify the subject or provide how-to information. A thriller written by Seichi Matsumoto in the late 1990s idealized Mount Fuji as the perfect suicide spot. The year the book was published, seventy bodies were found in or around the dormant volcano.

Undertakers and owners of American funeral homes earn frequent-flier miles every time they ship a corpse.

Casket companies in the United States have had to start building extra-large coffins in response to the 'super-sizing' of America.

Elephant graveyards have long been a part of the mythology of the animal kingdom. While elephants do not actually dig holes and bury their dead as humans do, they certainly exhibit clear signs of distress when they come upon the remains of one of their own.

Only a few other animals besides humans and elephants show any interest in their dead. Chimpanzees experience prolonged periods of grief, distress, and strange behavior in the presence of a dead social-mate or relative. They abandon the body only when it begins to decompose. A lion, on the other hand may sniff or lick at a dead lion, and then eat it.

Lions are not the biggest threat to humans wandering the jungles of Africa. Hippos kill many times more people than any other wild mammal on that continent.

Eagles make their nests at great heights, in mountains or treetops. The first baby eaglet to hatch will push all of its siblings out of the nest as they come out of their eggs. In this manner, all of the food the mother eagle brings will be only for the one that hatches first.

Sharks are voracious killers almost from the moment they are conceived. The largest shark foetus developing in its mother's womb will devour its smaller brothers and sisters so it won't have to share any of its food. Shark foetuses will also feed on the mother's steady supply of unfertilized eggs.

Thinning the Herd

❧

In any given year, fifteen times as many people are killed by falling coconuts than by sharks.

❧

On average, about twelve people die each year in Britain as a result of violent altercations with vending machines.

❧

A person will die from total lack of sleep sooner than from starvation.

❧

Skinny people who do not exercise are twice as likely to die prematurely than obese people who stay active.

❧

Since its opening in 1937, San Francisco's Golden Gate Bridge is by far the most popular suicide spot in the world. On average, one person takes a leap from the bridge every two weeks. Of the more than one thousand jumpers, fewer than thirty have lived to tell of the experience. Almost all of the survivors reported changing their minds the second they let go of the railing.

Hmm

❧

The beautiful Grand Canyon of Verdon in the lush south-eastern region of France attracts more than a million visitors a year. Some of them never leave. Since the building of barriers along the road in the 1980s, fewer people have been able to jump into the canyon or drive their cars off the cliffs, but they are finding it just as easy to take a leap off the nearby Artuby Bridge.

❧

Suicide rates increase dramatically under conservative governments. A recent study found that 35,000 more suicides occurred in Great Britain over the past hundred years whenever the Tories were in power.

❧

Myanmar has one of the world's strictest laws against the use of narcotics. Drug users can be punished by death for indulging in certain substances. In October 2000, that country's military junta declared caffeine to be a narcotic.

❧

In ancient China, women sometimes drank mercury heated in oil to deal with the pesky little problem of unwanted pregnancies. The potion was 100 percent effective in aborting foetuses, and more than 98 percent successful in killing the mothers.

⤳

On average, New York City recycling plants and trash-processing facilities find at least one dead body (or portion thereof) about every eighteen months.

⤳

At least nineteen people have been boiled to death in Yellowstone National Park since it opened in 1872. Many others have been seriously injured in the park's many hot springs. The overwhelming majority of these visitors jumped into the steaming pools trying to rescue their overly enthusiastic and not-too-bright dogs. Bear attacks and suicides also occur quite regularly at the park.

⤳

Throughout history, humans have considered suicide so abhorrent and frightening that nearly every culture has developed special ways of disposing of the corpses or ritualizing these deaths. In the eighteenth century, the English impaled the corpses with a stake and buried the bodies at a crossroads to confuse those unquiet spirits and keep them from coming back to life as vampires. In other European countries, the corpses of suicides were either set on fire, dragged through the streets, thrown in garbage heaps, or put in a barrel and dumped in a river.

Every year, *Forbes* magazine publishes a list of the world's richest dead celebrities. These were the lucky thirteen for 2006:

Kurt Cobain	$50 million
Elvis Presley	$42 million
Charles M. Schulz	$35 million
John Lennon	$24 million
Albert Einstein	$20 million
Andy Warhol	$19 million
Dr. Seuss	$10 million
Ray Charles	$10 million
Marilyn Monroe	$8 million
Johnny Cash	$8 million
J. R. R. Tolkien	$7 million
George Harrison	$7 million
Bob Marley	$7 million

Sources

I HAVE NEVER KILLED A MAN, BUT I HAVE READ
MANY OBITUARIES WITH A LOT OF PLEASURE.
Clarence Darrow (1857–1938)

EVERY EFFORT WAS made to authenticate the veracity of these stories. The overwhelming majority were checked against three or more legitimate news and reference sources, such as Associated Press, Reuters, *Encyclopaedia Britannica*. The very few that had only one or two verifiable references came directly from local newspaper accounts, academic or government reports, and encyclopedic or literary publications.

Some of the funniest and most interesting stories I found were originally posted on a variety of popular internet sites. Unfortunately, they were not all true, accurate or verifiable. I only included the ones that could be legitimately validated.

AAP General News (Australia)
ABC News
AboutVienna.org
Adoption.com
A&E Television Networks

Aerospaceweb.org

The Age (Melbourne, Australia, newspaper)

Alberta Report (Canada)

All Headline News

All Philosophy.com

American Experience (PBS)

American Transcendentalism Web (a biography of Henry David Thoreau in an online article by Ann Woodlief, Virginia Commonwealth University)

Amsterdam News (New York)

Ananova (UK)

Anecdotage.com

Answers.com

The Antioch Review

The Arab American News

Archive Photos.com

Arkansas Tonight (Online Radio and Politics)

Art Hazards News

Asbury Park Press (North Carolina)

Associated Press

Atlanta Journal-Constitution

Atlantis Rising magazine

The Australian (national newspaper)

Aviation History magazine

AZCentral.com (Arizona)

Bartleby's Quotes (Bartleby.com)

BBC News

Beliefnet.com

Belleville News-Democrat (Illinois)

Benjamin Franklin: A Biography by Ronald W. Clarke (2004)

The Best, Worst & Most Unusual by Bruce Felton and Mark Fowler (1994)

Billboard magazine

Biography Channel

The Birmingham Mail (England)

The Birmingham Post (England)

The Book of Scotland by William Chambers (1830)

Books and Writers (www.kirjasto.sci.fi)

Boston City Guide

The Boston Globe

Boston Herald

The Brussels Journal (Belgian newspaper)

Busca Biografias.com

Canadian Encyclopedia.com

Captain Cook Country (www.captaincook.org.uk)

Catholic Encyclopedia

Catholic Pilgrims.com

CBS News

CDC (Centers for Disease Control)

Celebrate Today.com

Celestis Space Services of America

Central Jersey *Home News Tribune*

CFW Enterprises.com

Channel 4 News (Jacksonville, Florida)

Channel 6 ABC News (Philadelphia)

ChicagoArtistsResource.org

Chicago Sun-Times

Chicago Tribune

China Daily (newspaper)

ChinaUnix.net

The Christian Century

The Cincinnati Post

Civil War Home.com

Classics at MIT

Clear Path International News

CNN

Columbia Encyclopedia

The Concise Oxford Dictionary of Quotations

Coney Island Museum

Cosmopolitan magazine

Court TV Crime Library

The Cromwell Association

Crosscurrents magazine

Cuisine du Monde

The Daily Breeze (Los Angeles)

The Daily Herald (Illinois)

The Daily Mail (London)

The Daily Mirror (London)

The Daily News (Los Angeles)

The Daily Post (Liverpool)

The Daily Press (Victorville, California)

The Daily Record (Glasgow, Scotland)

The Daily Telegraph (London)

Dave's Daily.com

Dead Musicians Directory

Death Penalty Information Center

De Telegraaf (Dutch newspaper)

Deutsche Presse-Agentur (German Press Agency)

The Dick Cavett Show

Discovery Channel

Dorset *Daily Echo*

Dutch News Service (Netherlands)

Dynamic Chiropractic newsletter

Early American Literature magazine

Earthview.com

Ebony magazine

The Economist

eHistory.com

8Notes.com

The 11th Armored Division Association

Encyclopaedia Britannica

Encyclopedia Americana (Grolier's)

ESPN

Esquire

The Evening Standard (London)

The Examiner (San Francisco)

Eyewitness to History.com

Fact Monster.com

Famous Last Words by Barnaby

Conrad (1961)

Fernbank Science Center (Atlanta, Georgia)

Find a Grave.com

Florida Museum of Natural History's International Shark Attack File

Folklore magazine

Forbes magazine

Fort Myers *News-Press*

Forward (New York newspaper)

Fox News (Australia)

Fox News (U.S.)

Gallup Poll

Gaudi Club (Barcelona)

Goodbye! magazine

Grizzly Man (documentary film)

Grove Concise Dictionary of Music

The Guardian (UK)

The Handbook of Texas Online

Harper's Magazine

The Heinz Family Philanthropies, 1994 Heinz Awards speech by
Teresa Heinz

Helena *Independent Record*

The Hindu (India)

Hinduism Today magazine

History of Funeral Customs by Wyoming Funeral Directors Association

A History of the Roman World from AD 138 to 337 by H. M. D. Parker
(London, 1958)

History Wired (Smithsonian Institution)

Houston Chronicle

The Humanist magazine

Humanities magazine

The Human Marvels.com

IMDB (Internet Movie Database)

The Independent (London)

Independent News & Media

The Independent on Sunday (London)

India Abroad.com

InfoPlease.com

Insight on the News

Interavia Business & Technology

International Cemetery and Funeral Association

International Herald Tribune

Ireland's Eye.com

The Journal (Newcastle, England)

The Journal of Criminal Law and Criminology

Journal of Neurosurgery

KHNL Channel 8 News (Hawaii)

Knight Ridder / Tribune

Knot magazine

Kyodo World News Service

The Last Days of Socrates by Plato (1993)

The Last Link on Left.com

Las Vegas Review-Journal

Lawlink (New South Wales Public Defender's Office)

Legacy Matters (www.estatevaults.com)

Lettres de Madame de Savigné (April 26, 1671)

Lewis Center for Educational Research

Lexington Herald-Leader (Kentucky)

Life magazine

Lincoln Journal Star (Nebraska)

The Literature Network

Liverpool Daily Post (UK)

Liverpool Echo (UK)

The Lives and Opinions of Eminent Philosophers by Diogenes Laertius (2006)

Lives of the Noble Greeks and Romans by Plutarch (AD 75)

Local London Network

London Free Press (Ontario, Canada)

Longview *News-Journal* (Texas)

Los Angeles Times

The Magazine Antiques

The Mail on Sunday (London)

Mammoth Cave National Park (official website)

Mark Twain A–Z by Kent Rasmussen (1996)

Messenger-Inquirer (Owensboro, Kentucky)

Miller Center of Public Affairs, University of Virginia

Milwaukee Journal Sentinel

The Mirror (London)

Mosaic (Winnipeg)

Most Haunted (Travel Channel television series)

MSNBC News Services

My Heart Is My Own by John Guy (2004)

NASA History Division

The Nashville News (Arkansas newspaper)

The Nation

National Catholic Reporter

The National Directory of Haunted Places by Dennis William Hauck (1994)

National Geographic

The National Park Service

National Parks magazine

National Review magazine

NBC News

New Music Classics.com

New Scientist

New Statesman magazine (UK)

New Straits Times

New York *Daily News*

New York Post

The New York Times

The New Zealand Herald

News Channel 3 (California)

The News Letter (Belfast, Northern Ireland)

News-Record (Piedmont Triad, North Carolina)

News24.com (South Africa)

Newsweek

Niagara Falls Daredevil Museum

North County Times (California)

Noticias Locas (Argentina)

November of the Soul: The Enigma of Suicide by George Howe Colt (2006)

NPR (National Public Radio)

The Oakland Tribune (California)

Ohio History Central Online Encyclopedia

Onstage magazine

Oops! by Paul Kirchner (1996)

Orkneyjar.com (Heritage of the Orkney Islands)

Orlando Sentinel (Florida)

The Oxford Dictionary of Byzantium

Oxford Student Publications

The Palm Beach Post (Florida)

PBS

The Pennsylvania Gazette

The People (London newspaper)

The Philadelphia Inquirer

Political Graveyard.com

Pope-Pourri by John Dollison (1994)

Proceso magazine (Madrid)

Psychology Journal

Sources

Quadrant magazine

Realm of St. Stephen: A History of Medieval Hungary by Pal Engel et al. (2001)

Real Premonitions (A&E television documentary)

Reason magazine

The Record (Bergen County, New Jersey)

ReefQuest Centre for Shark Research

The Register-Guard (Eugene, Oregon)

Reuters

The Review of Contemporary Fiction

Roadside America.com

Rocky Mountain News (Denver)

Rolling Stone magazine

The Sacramento Bee

The St. Petersburg Times (Florida newspaper)

Salidas de Emergencia by Eduardo Allende (2006)

Salon.com

The San Diego Union-Tribune

San Diego Zoo 'Animal Bytes'

San Francisco Chronicle

Scandinavian Studies magazine

Schott's Original Miscellany by Ben Schott (2003)

The Scotsman

Seattle Post-Intelligencer

The Seattle Times

The Sir Walter Raleigh Collection

Skeptical Inquirer magazine

SkyNews magazine

The Smoking Gun.com

Snopes.com

South Florida Sun-Sentinel

SouthPole.com

South Wales Echo (Cardiff)

Spiegel Online International News Service

The Star-Tribune (Minneapolis)

The Straight Dope.com

Studies in English Literature, 1500–1900 by David Stymeist (2004)

Stunt Players.com

Suddenly Senior.com

The Sun (UK)

The Sunday Mail (Glasgow, Scotland)

The Sunday Mercury (Birmingham, England)

The Sunday Mirror (London)

Swannanoa Valley Museum

The Swindon Advertiser (UK)

The Taipei Times

The Telegraph (India)

Texas Escapes Online Magazine

TexasScapes.com

Texas State Library and Archives Commission

Time magazine

The Times (Sydney, Australia)

The Times of India

The Times-Mirror (Los Angeles)

Times-News (Burlington, North Carolina)

Today in Science History (todayinsci.com)

Trivia-Library.com

TV.com

TVNZ (New Zealand)

The 20th Century by David Wallechinsky (1995)

Undiscovered Scotland

United Press International

University of Delaware

USA Today

US News & World Report

Vanity Fair magazine

Virginia Military Institute Archives

The Virginian-Pilot

The Wall Street Journal

Warsaw Times-Union (Indiana)

The Washington Post

The Washington Times

The Wave magazine

The Weekly Standard

The Western Mail (Cardiff, Wales)

The White House Online History Page

White Star Line Ships (official website)

Who Was Frank Silvera? by Garland Lee Thompson (online article at www.fsww.org/whois.html)

Wiltshire Times & Chippenham News (UK)

Windsor Star (Canada)

The Women's Review of Books

Worldwide Gourmet.com

WSB-TV News (Atlanta)

Wyoming Funeral Directors Association

Yellowstone National Park (official website)

If you enjoyed *Thinning the Herd* you'll love these other titles from Michael O'Mara:

The Book of
Senior Moments
by Shelley Klein

978-1-84317-164-5

Available at all good
bookshops, priced £9.99

More Senior Moments
(The Ones We Forgot)
by Shelley Klein

978-1-84317-256-7

Available at all good
bookshops, priced £9.99

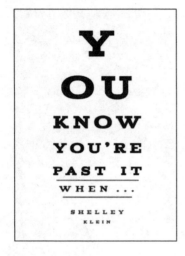

**You Know You're
Past It When . . .**
by Shelley Klein

978-1-84317-329-8

On sale October 2008,
priced £10

**The Seniors' Survival Guide:
New tricks for old dogs**
by Geoff Tibballs

978-1-84317-236-9

On sale October 2008,
priced £10